Figures of Speech

FIGURES
OF
SPEECH

60 ways
to turn a phrase
by Arthur Quinn

Hermagoras Press
Davis, California
1993

Published by Hermagoras Press
P.O. Box 1555, Davis, California 95617
Manufactured in the United States of America
by KNI Incorporated, Anaheim, California

Originally published 1982 by Gibbs Smith,
Publisher, Layton, Utah.   ISBN 0-87905-121-3.

ISBN 1-880393-02-6

The paper used in this publication meets the minimum requirements of
American National Standard for Information Sciences—Permanence of
Paper for Printed Library Materials, ANSI Z39,48-1984 ∞

And I must borrow every changing shape
to find expression.

T.S. ELIOT

Contents

Preface

ICAN STILL REMEMBER the occasion that started me thinking about writing this book. After having attended a stuffy academic convention, I impulsively decided to swing through New York to spend the evening with a friend who was then a writer for a weekly news magazine. I needed some fresh air.

I met him at his office on a Friday evening, the night the magazine is put to bed. Fortunately, by the time I arrived he had already finished his story for the week. Nonetheless, we had to wait for a while because his story was being submitted to the various reporters who had supplied him the information and had the right to suggest changes.

As he was scurrying in and out between phone conversations with them, he tossed a copy of his story to me, and announced "There is only one sentence I won't change." It was obviously a challenge from the journalist to the professor. When he returned a few minutes later, I read him the sentence. He was pleased; I'd gotten it right. "I thought the zeugma was particularly handsome," I said. Immediately his eyes glazed over and he reached for his coat. It was only a few hours later, after a pleasant dinner, that he finally asked, "All right, what the hell is a zeugma?"

What the hell *is* a zeugma? It is just a figure of speech, a rather witty one that I had never had the nerve to try. My friend had tried one just that day; and he knew he had written a nice sentence. What I knew was a name and definition that might help him isolate what was particularly striking about that sentence. This could be useful because sooner or later he

1

would find himself in a position where he might want to try another one. And, in fact, I could supply him with a series of famous zeugmas, from Shakespeare, the Bible, Alexander Pope. I wouldn't have to comment on these examples; he could see for himself the range of uses.

In one sense he already had a greater command of zeugmas than I did, for he had made one—I was learning from him. Zeugmas and the rest of the stylistic bestiary are of significance only insofar as they help us learn to write better. The professor learns from the journalist, and they both learn from Shakespeare. The figures are not essential in this process, but they can facilitate it.

Usually they do nothing of the kind. Usually they are hoarded as the arcane argot of the professional humanist. Graduate students in literature eagerly buy little dictionaries so that when a monograph intones about later Shakespeare's penchant for the anthimeria, they will have a place to look it up. So they look it up, while their own prose often becomes more and more like a monograph's, a groaning misery to read.

Writing is not like chemical engineering. We shouldn't learn the figures of speech the way we learn the periodic table of elements. We shouldn't because we are learning not about hypothetical structures in things, but about real potentialities within our language, within ourselves.

Learning about the figures of speech should be less like learning about the periodic table of elements than like learning how to model clay. To ask a sentence if it has a zeugma is not like asking a rock if it has silicon. In fact, the very phrase "figures of speech" is misleading in its static, passive form. It should be the "figurings of speech"—or, better yet, simply "figuring speech."

The figurings of speech reveal to us the apparently limitless plasticity of language itself. We are confronted, inescapably, with the intoxicating possibility that we can make language do for us almost anything we want. Or at least a Shakespeare can. The figures of speech help us to see how he does it, and how we might.

Therefore, in what follows, the quotations from Shakespeare, the Bible, and other sources are not presented to exemplify the definitions; the definitions are presented to lead to the quotations. And the quotations are there to show us how to do with language what we have not done before. They are there—must I confess?—for imitation.

I

To And or Not to And

ON THE NIGHT of June 21, 1932, Joe Jacobs, a professional prize fight manager, after hearing that his man had not been awarded the decision, achieved for himself linguistic immortality by shouting into the ring announcer's microphone, "We was robbed!"

"We" does not ordinarily go with "was." And we might think that Jacobs had simply made a grammatical mistake of a rather rudimentary kind. Yet, if he had said "were," he likely would have been consigned to the same oblivion as was the smug winning manager. Far from being a mistake, "was" was an inspiration. It was, to be more precise, an **enallage**, which is just the rhetorical name for an effective grammatical mistake.

There are literally hundreds of such names that have accumulated over the centuries, as generation after generation has striven to gain and give mastery over language. These figures of speech have been named and collected because they are, if used properly, extremely helpful in learning and teaching how to write, speak, read, listen, better. Writing is a matter of making linguistic choices, and reading depends upon understanding the linguistic choices made by someone else. The figures of speech help you see the choices available in a given context. And being able to see them helps you make them or judge them.

"We was robbed!" is a wonderfully effective complaint. As readers and writers, we would like to understand better why it is so effective. Not from a theoretical point of view. (Style, someone said, is like a frog; you can dissect the thing, but it somehow dies in the process.) Rather we want to understand it

5

concretely, practically. (Much as a naturalist would have understood that poor frog long before the vivisectionist got his hands on it.) In other words, we want to be able, when the occasion arises, to turn a phrase of similar effectiveness. As the magazine *Punch* did when it wrote, "You pays your money, and you takes your choice." Or as James Joyce did when he had Molly Bloom declare, "My patience are exhausted."

The romantics among us—or is it the romantic in each of us?—will complain that such phrases can be properly turned only in a moment of *true* inspiration, when we have lost our self-conscious, calculating natures, and thereby can express our authentic selves. Perhaps so, but at least we can prepare ourselves for those rare moments when lightning strikes.

Giving names to distinguishable features of style will not in and of itself bring about inspiration, or authenticity, or eloquence, or even mere competence. These are names, not incantations. The names will, however, allow us to juxtapose various effective passages which bear interesting resemblances one with another. From these juxtapositions, we can gain an actual sense why these passages are effective and how ours might be made more so.

The names in the end will fade before the richness of the examples, of language itself. In the end the names and definitions will proclaim their own inadequacy, much as in a wine tasting one is left with a sense of the inadequacy of the words connoisseurs use to describe the complexities of wine. Nonetheless, by the time you recognize the inadequacy of these viticultural descriptions, you have learned to discriminate between wines—and are able to decide for yourself if you like to drink sauterne with beef stew.

The simplest definition of a figure of speech is "an intended deviation from ordinary usage." (An intended deviation from ordinary grammatical usage is the specific figure of speech, enallage.) Here it will be the philosopher, not the romantic, who will be out to cause us trouble. "What, pray tell, *is* ordinary usage *really*? Must an intention be conscious? And how do you know a deviant when you see one?" If he wishes to flagellate himself with such questions, we will let him—while we get on with the mundane task of learning how to turn a phrase.

Let's cook a cheese omelet—or, rather, talk about cooking one. For ingredients we will need at least butter, eggs, and cheese. And we will also have to prepare these ingredients: melt the butter, whip the eggs, grate the cheese.

Ordinarily when we write about two or more items in a series or group, we use the single, simple conjunction "and" to connect them: eggs, cheese, and butter; melt, whip, and grate. Ordinarily, but not always. Sometimes we might decide to add another "and," as most cooks would add seasoning to my list of ingredients for a cheese omelet. Or we might try to omit it altogether, as I once tried to omit the step of grating the cheese.

The omission of an expected conjunction is called an **asyndeton**. Caesar is supposed to have said about Gaul: "I came, I saw, I conquered." Lincoln concluded the Gettysburg Address, "That government of the people, by the people, for the people, shall not perish from the earth."

Caesar seems to have omitted his conjunction to speed things up; he is emphasizing how quickly the conquest of a place follows from its being sighted by a great and ambitious general. Lincoln's omission is more subtle—or so it seems to me. Usually the items on a list are different but related things: eggs, butter, cheese. Sometimes they achieve a unity in which their distinctiveness is lost to all but the analytic mind, a good cheese omelet. Or perhaps we might even decide that they are but manifestations or expressions of the same thing. Lincoln would have us see these three aspects of government as constituting an inseparable whole. The asyndeton helps him do this.

Of course, these two distinguishable usages of asyndeton are not mutually exclusive. Lincoln's asyndeton contributes to the striking brevity of his address. And the psychoanalytically subtle among us will point out that at some level seeing is organically connected with conquering (and many other things as well). Nor are these two usages anything close to exhaustive.

There are a variety of reasons, and combinations of reasons, why one might choose to omit a conjunction. It is less important to try to classify these reasons than to taste some passages where the omission occurs.

The enemy said, I will pursue, I will overtake, I will divide the spoil; my lust shall be satisfied upon them; I will draw my sword, my hand shall destroy them. Thou didst blow with thy wind, the sea covered them: they sank as lead in the mighty waters.   Exod. 15:9*

I have spoken. You have heard; you know the facts; now give your decision.   Aristotle

The ring on the finger becomes thin beneath by wearing, the fall of dripping water hollows the stone.
                                                      Lucretius

I do not understand; I pause; I examine.
                                                      Montaigne

For God's sake, let us sit upon the ground
And tell sad stories of the death of kings:
How some have been depos'd, some slain in war,
Some haunted by the ghosts they have depos'd,
Some poison'd by their wives, some sleeping kill'd:
All murder'd   Shakespeare, R II 3.2.156**

In these examples, like those from Lincoln and Caesar, the asyndeton occurs in a series of clauses. But it can just as easily occur in a series of nouns.

For from within, out of the heart of men, proceed evil thoughts, adulteries, fornications, murders, thefts, covetous-

---

*Passages from the Bible are commonly abbreviated (see page 101) and the citation marks the chapter and beginning verse number of the quotation and does not include subsequent verse citations even if used in the quotation.

**Passages from the works of William Shakespeare are commonly abbreviated as to their source (see page 101); and, again, line citations designate only the beginning line of the quotation even when more than one line is quoted.

ness, wickedness, deceit, lasciviousness, an evil eye, blasphemy, pride, foolishness: All these evil things come from within, and defile the man. Mark 7:21

And now abideth faith, hope, charity, these three; but the greatest of these is charity. 1 Cor. 13:13

O mighty Caesar! dost thou lie so low?
Are all thy conquests, glories, triumphs, spoils,
Shrunk to this little measure?
Shakespeare, JC 3.1.148

O! what a noble mind is here o'er-thrown: The courtier's, soldier's, scholar's, eye, tongue, sword.
Ham. 3.1.159

Peace is not an absence of war, it is a virtue, a state of mind, a disposition for benevolence, confidence, justice.
Spinoza

A gentle breeze entering through the windows, always flung wide open, brought into the bare room the softness of the sky, the languor of the earth, the bewitching breath of the Eastern waters. Conrad

It can occur between verbs, prepositional phrases, or adjectives.

A woman mov'd is like a fountain troubled,
Muddy, ill-seeming, thick, bereft of beauty.
Shakespeare, TS 5.2.143

All hail, great master! Grave sir, hail! I come
To answer thy best pleasure; be't to fly,
To swim to dive into the fire, to ride
On the curl'd clouds. Tem. 1.2.189

The unplumbed, salt, estranging sea. Arnold

We see these beautiful co-adaptations...only a little less plainly in the humblest parasite which clings to the hairs of a quadruped or feathers of a bird; in the structure of the beetle which dives through the water; in the plumed seed which is wafted by the gentlest breeze Darwin

It can occur more than once.

Eros is bold, enterprising, strong, a mighty hunter, always
weaving some intrigue or other, keen in the pursuit of wisdom,
fertile in resources; a philosopher at all times, terrible as an
enchanter, sorcerer, sophist.   Plato

Hoo! hearts, tongues, figures, scribes, bards, poets, cannot
Think, speak, cast, write, sing, number— hoo! —
His love to Antony.
                                          Shakespeare, A & C 3.2.16

An asyndeton can occur within a sentence anywhere—at
the beginning, at the end.

A cathedral, a wave of a storm, a dancer's leap, never turn
out to be as high as we had hoped.   Proust

A confidence always aims at glory, scandal, excuse,
propaganda.   Valéry

Sometimes one element of the series will stand out, but
usually not.

A sad thing is a wolf in the fold, rain on ripe corn, wind in
the trees, the anger of Amaryllis.   Virgil

I am a Jew. Hath not a Jew eyes? Hath not a Jew hands,
organs, dimensions, senses, affections, passions?
                                          Shakespeare, MV 3.1.62

Like all figures of speech, the asyndeton has its risks.
Too frequent use of the asyndeton, for instance, will give to
prose a jerky, unconnected feel; the prose of Seneca was once
criticized as "sand without lime." To avoid this problem some
of the above passages make explicit—through either a concluding or introductory summary—why the series is an
organic whole.

Strange to say, at least one passage above achieved the
typical effect of an asyndeton without actually omitting a
conjunction. This is just one of those cases in which rhetorical
practice can cause consternation for the poor philosopher. "Is

that an asyndeton?" It is and it isn't. "Aren't you in saying that violating the law of contradiction?" I are and I aren't.

Contradiction is not a hobgoblin for most of us, particularly in our ordinary use of language. If something works rhetorically, its contrary will probably work as well. If not having enough conjunctions is effective, then so also will be having too many. Choosing to have too many conjunctions is to make a **polysyndeton**.

Sometimes the polysyndeton gives the sense of an ever lengthening catalogue of roughly equal members.

> And Joshua, and all Israel with him, took Achan the son of Zerah, and the silver, and the garment, and the wedge of gold, and his sons, and his daughters, and his oxen, and his asses, and his sheep, and his tent, and all that he had.
>
> Josh.7:24

> These things let us thoroughly know—that the man is our enemy, and has spoiled us of our dominions, and for a length of time has insulted us, and that all things whatever which at any time we hoped others would do for us are found against us; and that all the things which remain must be found in our own very selves; and that if we will not fight him there, here it is likely we may be forced to fight him.
>
> Demosthenes

> Unless hours were cups of sack, and minutes capons, and clocks the tongues of bawds, and dials the signs of leaping houses, and the blessed sun himself a fair hot wench in flame-color'd taffeta, I see no reason why thou shouldst be so superfluous to demand the time of the day.
>
> Shakespeare, 1 H IV 1.2.7

> How all the other passions fleet to air,
> As doubtful thoughts, and rash-
> embrac'd despair,
> And shuddering fear, and green-ey'd
> jealousy.   MV 3.2.105

Sometimes the series moves from the less important to the more important, sometimes from the general to the specific.

Whatever this is that I am, it is a little flesh and breath and
the ruling part.   Marcus Aurelius

When you are old and gray and full of sleep,
And nodding by the fire, take down this book.

Yeats

More often, the elements are related spatially or tem-
porally.

And they came to the place which God had told him of; and
Abraham built an altar there, and laid the wood in order, and
bound Isaac his son, and laid him on the altar upon the wood.
And Abraham stretched forth his hand, and took the knife to
slay his son. And the Angel of the Lord called unto him out of
heaven, and said, Abraham, Abraham: and he said, Here am I.

Gen. 22:9

My sheep hear my voice, and I know them, and they follow
me: And I give unto them eternal life; and they shall never
perish.   John 10:27

When men drink, then they are rich and successful and win
lawsuits and are happy and help their friends. Quickly, bring
me a beaker of wine.   Aristophanes

The horizon narrowed and widened, and dipped and rose,
and at all times its edge was jagged with waves that seemed
thrust up in points like rocks.   Crane

For some two centuries, perhaps, Town Hill had stood with
its plank-built Georgian Church in the middle of the village
green, and with the houses round the church, and with the
orchards beyond the houses, and with the corn-fields stretching
away beyond the fruit trees...The desertion of Town Hill was
not a paradox after all; it was of one piece with the great
human enterprise which had founded and peopled Cincinnati
and Chicago and Denver and San Francisco.

Toynbee

It has been often noted that the indefiniteness of "and"
envelops biblical narratives, such as the story of Abraham and
Isaac, in mystery. Occasionally, in the Bible and elsewhere,
repeated polysyndetons have an almost hypnotic power.

And I stood upon the sand of the sea, and saw a beast rise up out of the sea, having seven heads and ten horns, and upon his horns ten crowns, and upon his heads the name of blasphemy. And the beast which I saw was like unto a leopard, and his feet were as the feet of a bear, and his mouth as the mouth of a lion: and the dragon gave him his power, and his seat, and great authority. And I saw one of his heads as it were wounded to death; and his deadly wound was healed: and all the world wondered after the beast.

Rev. 13:1

She is older than the rocks among which she sits; like the vampire, she has been dead many times, and learned the secrets of the grave; and has been a diver in deep seas, and keeps their fallen day about her; and trafficked for strange webs with Eastern merchants: and as Leda, was the mother of Helen of Troy, and, as Saint Anne, the mother of Mary; and all this has been to her but as the sound of lyres and flutes, and lives only in the delicacy with which it has molded the changing lineaments, and tinged the eyelids and the hands.

Pater

Taken together, the above quotations show, more than any argument could, how useful polysyndeton is. As an asyndeton can hurry us along, so the polysyndeton can slow us down, thereby adding dignity to what we say, much like the slow motion of a ceremony. Or, rather than dignity, it can convey an author's own impatience with the list—he thinks it's very long too.

One frequent use of polysyndeton is simply beginning a sentence with an apparently unnecessary conjunction. This can give a dignified rhythm to the sentence. Or, contrarily, it can make the sentence seem more colloquial, as if the writer were stringing together sentences the way most of us do in ordinary conversation. So much for the law of contradiction.

And one can, of course, use other conjunctions than "and." So frequent is the polysyndeton of "or" or "nor" that one nineteenth-century handbook, taking liberties with traditional usage, suggested assigning to it the name **paradiastole**.

But the seventh day is the sabbath of the Lord thy God: in it thou shalt not do any work, thou, nor thy son, nor thy

daughter, thy manservant, nor thy maidservant, nor thy cattle,
nor thy stranger that is within thy gates.

Exod. 20:10

There is no man that hath left house, or parents, or
brethren, or wife, or children, for the Kingdom of God's sake,
who shall not receive manifold more in this present time, and
in the world to come life everlasting.

Luke 18:29

Not snow, no, nor rain, nor heat, nor night keeps them
from accomplishing their appointed courses with all speed.

Herodotus

He who greatly excels in beauty, strength, birth, or wealth,
and he, on the other hand, who is very poor, or very weak, or
very disgraced, find it difficult to follow rational principles.

Aristotle

Neither men nor gods nor bookstalls have ever allowed
poets to be mediocre.   Horace

For I have neither wit, nor words, nor worth,
Action, nor utterance, nor the power of speech,
To stir men's blood: I only speak right on.

Shakespeare, JC 3.2.225

That time of year thou mayst in me behold
When yellow leaves, or none, or few, do hang
Upon those boughs which shake against the cold.

S 73.1

O! that I were as great
As is my grief, or lesser than my name,
Or that I could forget what I have been,
Or not remember what I must be now.

R II 3.3.136

Why make so much of fragmentary blue
In here and there a bird, or butterfly,
Or flower, or wearing-stone, or open eye,
When heaven presents in sheets the solid hue?

Frost

The visitor to the Louvre knows that he will not find the
great English artists significantly represented there — nor

Goya, nor Michaelangelo (as painter), nor Piero della Francesca, nor Grunewald. Malraux

Although most writers will tend to prefer either asyndeton or polysyndeton in their figurative play with conjunction—Shakespeare prefers asyndeton, the Bible poly—there is no reason that both cannot be employed, even in the same sentence. Sometimes this seems to be done simply for the sake of variety as when Thomas Merton writes: "And so it was with me. Books and ideas and poems and stories, pictures and music, buildings, cities, places, philosophies were to be the materials on which grace would work." But sometimes the effects are more subtle.

And as it was in the days of Noah so shall it be also in the days of the Son of man. They did eat, they drank, they married wives, they were given in marriage, until the day that Noah entered into the ark, and the flood came, and destroyed them all. Luke 17:26

As long as rivers shall run down to the sea, or shadows touch the mountain slopes, or stars graze in the vault of heaven, so long shall your honor, your name, your praises endure. Virgil

Ay, so thou dost,
Italian fiend!—Ay me, most credulous fool,
Egregious murderer, thief, anything
That's due to all villains past, in being,
To come. O! give me cord, or knife, or poison,
Some upright justicer....
Spit and throw stones, cast mire upon me set
The dogs o' the street to bay me; every villain
Be called Posterumus Leonatus; and
Be villainy less than 'twas! O Imogen!
My queen, my life, my wife! O Imogen!
Imogen, Imogen.
Shakespeare, Cym. 5.5.210

I confess that sometimes long catalogues affect me like an asyndeton so that when the "and" finally occurs it is unexpected; for example, a sentence from Aristophanes: "Mankind, fleet of life, like tree leaves, weak creatures of clay, unsubstantial as shadows, wingless, ephemeral, wretched, mortal and dreamlike." You see what happens when you study the figures of speech too long.

Perhaps now is the best moment—with me neurasthenically over-sensitive and you skeptical—for me to introduce you to a truly exotic combination of words, the hendiadys.

In any sentence some words seem more equal than others. The noun seems more equal than the adjective, the adjective than the article. When I admonish you "Try to add the eggs to the bubbling butter just before it would start to burn," the word "add" does seem dependent upon the word "try." Yet "add" is what you are going to do. And so in our ordinary speech we will instinctively want to make "add" equal to "try." We often will say not "try to add," but "try and add." Mae West did not say "Come up to see me sometime."

We can say "nice and warm" when we mean "nicely warm" yet want to emphasize not that it is warm but that it is nice. And when in the Old Testament the Lord God wants to punish a large group of people, He sometimes dumps on them burning sulphur; for His purposes the sulphur is incidental, the burning essential. Hence, burning sulphur becomes fire and brimstone.

These usages are examples of what we call the hendiadys. **Hendiadys** is a peculiar form of polysyndeton in which "and" is used to split a single thing into two, or even three. When Jesus said "I am the Way, the Truth, and the Life," perhaps what was meant was, "I am the true and living Way." And when the Lord God announces to Eve that He will "greatly multiply thy sorrow and thy conception," He is clearly referring to her conceiving sorrow—namely, the pains of childbirth.

I love the Lord, because he hath heard my voice and my supplications.   Ps. 116:1

For thine is the kingdom, and the power, and the glory, for ever. Amen.   Matt. 6:13

By force and arms   Caesar

Revenge and satisfaction....his hapless hand and blow
....posterity and infamy   Tacitus

It is a tale
Told by an idiot, full of sound and fury,
Signifying nothing.   Shakespeare, Mac. 5.5.26

The heaviness and the guilt within my bosom
Takes off my manhood.   Cym. 5.2.1

But in the gross and scope of my opinion,
This bodes some strange eruption to our state.
                                                Ham. 1.1.68

Up! up! my friend, and clear your looks;
Why all this toil and trouble?   Wordsworth

Polysyndeton, asyndeton, paradiastole, hendiadys—
just names that help us appreciate the flexibility, the opportunities in what might appear to us to be entirely uninteresting
words, the conjunctions. What was bland before now has
texture and taste.

II.

Effective Misspelling

W E HAVE TREATED the asyndeton-polysyndeton group of figures at length because they provide a good introduction to the figures in general. What we now require is a way to systematically survey the full range of the figures. This is provided by another group of figures, intrinsically perhaps the least interesting of all, the figures of **metaplasmus**. You have used a metaplasmic figure when you have purposely misspelled.

Such figures are really quite common, common but trivial. They are common, for instance, in the permutations to which first names are subjected. Edward can become Ward or Ed; Ed can become Eddie or Ted; Ted can become Teddy or Tad. The shortening of a name implies a familiarity; the addition of an -ie or -y adds also the sense of a diminutive or perhaps affection. On the other hand, what an Edward is called might depend upon what sounds best with his last name; an Edward Bond might be called Ward, but an Edward Kennedy would more likely be a Teddy.

This pattern is repeated in the handling of other words. If we wish to emphasize the sounds of a dialect, we might misspell God as Gawd. If we wish to emphasize His apparent impotence in our world, we might,with Samuel Beckett, add a diminutive to make Him Godot. If on the other hand we are concerned about offending Him when we curse, we might rearrange His name into something more mundane, and mutter, "Dog gone it," or "Dog nab it." (Or perhaps we can with Benjamin Jowett make a profound point, and translate Plato's "Good" as our "God," by a simple if calculated misspelling.)

This is all clear enough. It becomes clearer still if we try to reduce the above changes in Edward and God to a limited number of operations. To reduce Edward to Ed is to omit part of the name. To change Ed to Ted is to add to it. To change Ted to Tad is to substitute one letter for another. And, finally, to make a god into a dog is to change the arrangement of the letters. These are the four possible ways to misspell—by addition, omission, substitution, or arrangement. (We could even try to be more elegant by defining substitution and arrangement as changes which combine addition and omission—but, like most attempts at elegance, this is more trouble than it's worth.)

These four modes of deviating from ordinary spelling are also the four basic modes of deviating from ordinary usage generally. We will classify the figures of speech as either figures of addition, omission, substitution or arrangement. Hence the first question we will ask of any interesting turn of phrase, any figure of speech, is how does it play with, turn away from, deviate from, twist, figure ordinary usage. How? Asyndeton omits. Polysyndeton and paradiastole add. Hendiadys...ah, hendiadys is, as usual, not quite so simple. To understand it we need more questions.

An obvious second question to ask is "Where?" In our misspellings of Edward, where have we omitted? From the beginning? Ward. From the end? Ed. Where have we added? On the end? Eddie At the beginning? Ted. Where have we substituted? In the middle? Tad. Thus, this second question— Where?—does give us an adequate system for classifying the permutations of Edward. But this is not always the most useful second question to ask.

For instance, in the case of the asyndeton-polysyndeton group it is certainly not the most useful question to ask. With this group, "What?" is a more important question. What are being added or omitted? Conjunctions. The addition of a conjunction is a polysyndeton. The addition of the particular conjunction "or" or "nor" is the particular form of polysyndeton, the paradiastole.

If we are fastidious in our classification of asyndetons, we might want to further discriminate on the basis of the question "Where?" Some handbooks suggest that we distinguish the omission of a conjunction between phrases or words— **brachylogia**—from the omission between clauses—the asyndeton proper. This distinction seems to me to be too nice to be of any use. And this point is an important one.

The danger in a classification system such as this is that, like the robot which turns upon and begins to dictate to its maker, it can become an end in itself. The system will have served its purpose not when it is "complete" (whatever that means), but when it can be dispensed with. Its function is partial and temporary. We are not going to follow in the footsteps of the Sorcerer's Apprentice.

In general, we will find the question "How?" helpful in tasting a phrase. "Where?" or "What?" sometimes will be. "Where?" *and* "What?" rarely will. These simple questions— How? Where? What?—can guide us through the jungle of style, until the day we find our own individual ways.

To see these questions working in practice let us look at the metaplasmic figures. Here the admitted triviality is an advantage. This once, we will not mind if the figures serve the system. (Perhaps I should add that I have given the names only to show that I am systematizing customary distinctions. I would expect no one, except a fool or a scholar, to want to learn them—and perhaps not even the fool.)

How? Addition. Where? Beginning. The figure? **Prosthesis**.

I hold you as a thing enskied and sainted.
Shakespeare, MM 1.4.34

I all alone beweep my outcast state. S 29.1

Addition to the middle: **epenthesis**.

Lie blist'ring fore the visiting sun TNK 1.1.146

Give Mutius burial with our bretheren
Tit. 1.1.348

Addition to the end: **proparalepsis**.

And even the life precurse of feared events...
Have heaven and earth together demonstrated
Unto our climature and countrymen.
Shakespeare, Ham. 1.1.121

I can call spirits from the vasty deep.
I H IV 3.1.52

Subtraction from the beginning: **aphaearesis**.

The king hath cause to plain
Shakespeare, KL 3.1.39

Use every man after his desert, and who should 'scape
whipping?   Ham. 2.2.561

Subtraction from the middle: **syncope**.

Thou thy worldy task hast done,
Home art gone, and ta'en thy wages.
Shakespeare, Cym. 4.2.258

Your lordship, though not clean past your youth, hath yet
some smack of age in you, some relish of the saltness of time.
2 H IV 1.2.112

Subtraction from the conclusion: **apocope**.

If I might in entreaties find success—
As seld I have the chance—I would desire
My famous cousin to our Grecian tents.
Shakespeare, T&C 4.5.148

I am Sir Oracle,
And when I ope my lips let no dog bark!
MV 1.1.93

The elimination of a vowel to contract two words into
one is so common—don't, it's—that it is the one figure of
metaplasmus in which "What?" not "Where?" is the dis-
tinguishing second question. The omission of a vowel in a
contraction is a **synaloepha**.

Take't; 'tis yours. What is't?

> Shakespeare, Cor. 1.9.80

Win us with honest trifles, to betray's
In deepest consequence.   Mac. 1.3.123

Substitutions or rearrangements of spelling are far rarer than additions or omissions, even in Shakespeare. The danger of misunderstanding is far greater, as anyone who has tried to work out an acrostic will attest. Hence the terminology is simpler. All substitutions are **antisthecons**.

Or, ere they meet, in me, O nature, cesse!

> Shakespeare, AW 5.3.75

Come, go we then togither.   T&C 1.1.120

Rearrangements are **metatheses**.

With liver burning hot. Frevent.   MWW 2.1.122

A cestron Brimm'd with the blood of men   TNK 5.1.46

We can, of course, combine metaplasmic figures. If Shakespeare's name for his ignoble savage, Caliban, is really a play on cannibal, then perhaps we have a syncopic metathesis. But this pales before Spenser's contraction of "would not" into "nould"—a synaloephaic metathesis, metaplasmically speaking, of course.

Our system for classification will begin to degenerate into esoteric silliness the moment we forget the reason we have developed it in the first place. And to remember this we must always remember to ask of our figures the most important question of all—not how, not where, not what, but why. *Why* does an author or speaker choose to turn a phrase in a particular way?

Our system of classification cannot of itself answer the question why. But it will help us, perhaps even force us, to ask *why* more frequently than we would earlier have thought possible. A writer who is going to use a conjunction and then begins to think about omitting it, or using more than one, will not find the choice made for him by his knowledge of figures. The figures have done their work when they have made richer the choices he perceives. It enhances his freedom, and thereby invites him to reflect more deeply on why *he* is writing.

Once again the triviality of the metaplasmic figures is initially useful for the sake of clarity. Choices which are almost overwhelming in their richness with regard to other groups of figures are plainer here. Why does Shakespeare choose to misspell? Usually it is simply for the sake of sound—to help the rhythm or rhyme, or to convey a colloquial tone. Nonetheless, sometimes he seems to have more in mind.

When in *Hamlet* he uses "climature," he seems to want to suggest both "climate" and "temperature." When he has Cleopatra as she grasps the asp speak of the "knot intrinsicate of life," he does seem to be suggesting both "intrinsic" and "intricate." When Portia speaks of the quality of mercy not being "strained," few will recognize this as a metaplasmus at all; lopping off the first syllable of "constrained" so enriches the word that we are prepared to do without the primary meaning entirely.

So perhaps we can crudely distinguish between metaplasmic figures which improve the sound and those which complicate the sense. This distinction, despite its roughness, can help us see the point of usages which otherwise might seem just strange. Lewis Carroll has Humpty Dumpty explain to Alice (and to us) that when he uses the word "slithy" he means both "sly" and "lithe." Thereby, Carroll has given to us an insight into his own practice and that of other "nonsense" writers as well. And we don't need Carroll to explain to us what Disraeli meant when he spoke of "anecdotage." And it is not far from Humpty Dumpty and anecdotage to that Irish wag of genius, James Joyce. In *Ulysses* Joyce uses all the metaplasmic figures (and virtually all the other figures as well). But it is in his *Finnegans Wake* that misspelling achieves its apotheosis into a dominant literary technique. (Even the most trivial figures, it seems, are not so trivial, after all.)

Let me compose for you a sentence containing just a few of the spelling mistakes to be found on the first few pages of this work. "After giving the cropse of his wife a decent funferall, the man, really a fornicationist at heart, sinduced his daughter into an act of insect." To read such a sentence is to watch Thought plunge into the sea of words and come up half-drowned. It is to realize that despite all the comfort grammarians, logicians, and spelling bee judges benevolently try to offer us, language is a sea which sloshes, to quote Joyce, "somewhere, parently, in the ginnandgo gap between antediluvious and annadominant."

I suspect that a few readers, despite my efforts to distract them with metaplasmus, Charles Dodgson, and James Joyce, are still waiting for me to define "hendiadys." I fear even a pious attendance at Finnegan's wake cannot save me from the task.

A **hendiadys** is the addition of a conjunction between an adjective and a noun, accompanied usually by the rearrangement of the order of the adjective and noun, and always by the substitution of a noun for the adjective. Have I left anything out?

Oh, yes. I seem to hear a reader saying that I have omitted an explanation of how this definition fits such a common hendiadys as "try and do." Well, I guess "try and do" isn't a hendiadys *really*. Certainly my definition is too elegant to be wrung.

III

Missing Links and
Headless Horsemen

THE DANGERS OF OMISSION are obvious enough. The reader will fail to fill in the blank—or will fill it improperly. Few people who read for the first time Isaiah 38:12 will be able to supply the omission, or perhaps even to see where it occurs. "Mine age is departed, and is removed from me as a shepherd's tent: I have cut off like a weaver my life." It is only when you think about the weaver that you begin to suspect something has been omitted, that the last part of the verse should have its analogy filled out a bit. "I have cut off my life as a weaver cuts off his threads." The author has assumed that his readers know more about weaving than most of us do now. Hence the danger of this omission.

What one reader will find obvious another will find difficult. What to one culture is elegant economy, or even just normal expression, to another can be enigmatic brevity or even perverse obscurity. Such a cultural difference makes the King James Bible, at least as it was originally printed, a wonderful source for the study of **ellipsis**, the general name given to the figure of omission. In many respects ancient Hebrew and Greek were far more economical than English. Thus the King James translators felt obliged to supply some of the omissions. To guide the reader, they had these additions printed in italics.

And they came unto Jacob their father unto the land of Canaan, and told him all that befell unto them; saying The man, *who is* the lord of the land, spake roughly to us, and took us for spies of the country. And we said unto him, We *are* true

27

men; we are no spies: We *be* twelve brethren, sons of our father; one *is* not, and the youngest *is* this day with our father in the land of Canaan. And the man, the lord of the country, said unto us, Hereby shall I know that ye *are* true *men;* leave one of your brethren *here* with me, and take *food for* the famine of your households, and be gone: And bring your youngest brother unto me: then shall I know that ye *are* no spies, but *that* ye *are* true *men:* so will I deliver you your brother, and ye shall traffic in the land.   Gen. 42.29

Although English is not nearly as fruitful a language for ellipsis as either Hebrew or Greek, ellipsis is still an extremely important stylistic device. The most common forms of it are, quite naturally, the safest. What more easily supplied than an omitted conjunction, and what more common figure of ellipsis than asyndeton? Nonetheless, if we can almost always omit conjunctions safely, sometimes we can nouns or verbs or whole prepositional phrases.

For a day in thy courts is better than a thousand. I had rather be a doorkeeper in the house of my God, than to dwell in the tents of wickedness.   Ps. 84:10

And he commanded the multitude to sit down on the grass, and took the five loaves, and the two fishes, and looking up to heaven, he blessed, and brake, and gave the loaves to his disciples, and his disciples to the multitude.
                                    Matt. 14:19

Of a criminal, it is the part to die, sentenced by law; but of a general—fighting with his country's foes.
                                    Demosthenes

So Judas did to Christ: but he, in twelve,
Found truth in all but one; I, in twelve thousand, none.
                                    Shakespeare, R II 4.1.170

And when he's old, cashier'd.

                                    O 1.1.48

Haply you shall not see me more; or if,
A mangled shadow.
                                    A&C 4.2.26

Men who cherish for women the highest respect are seldom
popular with.   Addison

Don't throw stones at your neighbors' if your own
windows are glass.   Franklin

For the butterfly, mating and propagation involve the
sacrifice of life; for the human, the sacrifice of beauty.
                                                                  Goethe

Everybody's friend is nobody's.   Schopenhauer

"We are waiting for the long-promised invasion. So are
the fishes." No one will find it difficult to supply what the fishes
are waiting for in this piece of Churchillian bluster. They, like
"we," are waiting for the long-promised invasion. The ellipsis
here is really only relative because the omitted phrase appears
in the passage elsewhere. Sometimes ellipsis can be more
complicated.

Take, for example, Byron's "Let us have wine and
women, mirth and laughter/Sermons and soda water the
morrow." Byron doesn't want his wine with soda, nor his
women with sermons. He wants the sermons and soda
tomorrow, the women and wine tonight—first he'll sin, then
convalesce. We have to realize that the omitted material
contrasts with its parallel in the passage. This is to expect more
from the reader, and can be risky.

"God judgeth the righteous, and God is angry every day."
This verse from Psalm 7 is a little jarring to our sense of fair
play. It would not be a very nice God who was unceasingly
angry even at the righteous. The King James version solves this
problem by interpreting the verse as a piece of contrastive
ellipsis, "God judgeth the righteous, and God is angry *with the
wicked* every day."

The relative ellipsis of a verb is called a **zeugma**, the figure
of speech with which I annoyed my journalist friend. One verb
is left to govern a number of clauses.

Out of Zion shall go forth the law, and the word of the
Lord from Jerusalem.   Isa. 2.3

But passion lends them power, time means, to meet.

Shakespeare, R & J 2. Prol. 13

How Tarquin wronged me, I Collatine.   RL 819

As you on him Demetrius dote on you!

MND 1.1.225

Histories make men wise; poets, witty; the mathematics, subtile; natural philosophy, deep; moral, grave; logic and rhetoric, able to contend.   Bacon

One leaf she lays down, a floor of granite; then a thousand ages, and a bed of slate; a thousand ages, and a measure of coal; a thousand ages, and a layer of marl and mud; vegetable forms appear; her first misshapen animals, zoophyte, trilobium.

Emerson

One will rarely err if extreme actions be ascribed to vanity, ordinary actions to habit, and mean actions to fear.

Nietzsche

These ellipses are simple enough (except perhaps for the example from Bacon). In each the expressed verb is supplied to the other clauses needing one. (With Bacon you need the verb and its object.) Things are not quite so simple with the following zeugmas.

And all the people saw the thunderings, and the lightnings, and the noise of the trumpet, and the mountain smoking.

Exod. 20:18

A woman takes off her claim to respect along with her garments.

Herodotus

Waging war and peace   Sallust

Let's have a dance ere we are married, that we may lighten our own hearts and our wives' heels

Shakespeare, MAAN 5.4

Neither the sun nor death can be regarded steadily.

La Rochfoucauld

Or stain her Honour, or her new Brocade...
Or lose her Heart, or Necklace at a Ball...
Not louder Shrieks to pitying Heav'ns are cast,
When Husbands or when Lap-dogs breathe their last.

                                                        Pope

Although in each of the above we can supply the same verb to each of the needy clauses or objects, the verb is not exactly the same—these ellipses are contrastive in the sense that we are contrasting two meanings of the same word. We do not look at the sun and death in the same sense, nor do we see lightning and thunder similarly. These zeugmas are parallel in form but contrastive in meaning.

Some handbooks wish to restrict the term zeugma to ellipses which are of this type. Others prefer to keep the general term zeugma for ellipses of verbs, and call the others **syllepses**. This confusion has persisted through the centuries because most syllepses are zeugmas, while the most striking zeugmas are syllepses. Example of a syllepsis which is not a zeugma: "Bad prose, like cholera, is a communicable disease."

Some ellipses are even more extreme than either the parallel or contrastive types. The reader must supply the omitted material without the direct textual assistance which is provided in the other forms. **Absolute ellipsis** is the rhetorical name given for Caesar's last words ("Et tu, Brute."), Poe's refrain ("only this, and nothing more"), and the Queen of Hearts' expression of displeasure ("Off with his head!"). Dorothy Parker could even employ one to express her disagreement with Byron's disjunction of alcohol and religion: "Three high balls and I think I'm Saint Francis of Assisi."

Every man to his city, and every man to his own country.
                                                        1 Kings 22:36

The burden of Tyre. Howl, ye ships of Tarshish; for it is laid waste.   Isa. 23:1

Glory to God in the highest, and on earth peace, good will toward men.   Luke 2:14

Meats for the belly, and the belly for meats: but God shall
destroy both it and them.   1 Cor. 6:13

O eyes, no eyes, but fountains fraught with tears;
O life, no life, but lively form of death;
O world, no world, but mass of public wrongs,
Confused and filled with murder and misdeeds.

                                                              Kyd

For what, alas, can these my single arms? What propugna-
tion is in one man's valour?
                                      Shakespeare, T&C 2.2.135

I your commission will forthwith dispatch
And he to England shall along with you

                                                      Ham. 3.3.3

What! all my pretty chickens and their dam
At one fell swoop?   Mac. 4.3.216

Wisely and slow; they stumble that run fast.

                                                    R&J 2.3.94

No arts; no letters; no society; and which is worst of all,
continual fear and danger of violent death; and the life of man,
solitary, poor, nasty, brutish, and short.

                                                            Hobbes

Happy the people whose annals are boring to read.
                                                      Montesquieu

The head Sublime, the heart Pathos, the genitals Beauty,
the hands and feet Proportion.   Blake

The great tragedy of science—the slaying of a beautiful
hypothesis by an ugly fact.   T.H. Huxley

Nearing the end of his tether now. Sober serious man with a
bit of the savings-bank I'd say. Wife a good cook and washer.
Daughter working the machine in the parlour. Plain Jane, no
damn nonsense.   Joyce

After such knowledge, what forgiveness?   Eliot

No tears in the writer, no tears in the reader.   Frost

Prayers are not heard. Basalt and granite.
Above them, a bird of prey. The only beauty.
Thin-lipped, blue-eyed, without grace or hope,
Before God the Terrible, body of the world.

                                                                   Milosz

The most daring of such absolute ellipses are those which leave the sentence entirely without a verb. Such an intended sentence fragment is called a **scesis onamaton**. And perhaps I should correct myself about calling it daring, for in the twentieth century the scesis onamaton has become a conventional way to indicate either the apprehension of immediate particulars or the flow of consciousness. What was once fresh, almost overpowering, in its directness now seems staid, even mannered. Such as Sandburg's "Hog butcher for the world/Tool maker, stacker of wheat,/Player with railroads and the nation's freight handler;/Stormy, husky, brawling,/City of the big shoulders."

So far we have been focussing our attention on the omission of the single word or phrase. Sometimes one can intelligibly omit more than a phrase. This is easiest done when the omitted clause is a premise which can be logically inferred from our argument. When we say that Socrates is mortal because he is a man, we can expect that it will be realized we are assuming (but not saying) that all men are mortal. Such a logical use of omission is called an **enthymeme.**

Timon: Why dost thou call them knaves? Thou know'st them
    not.
Apemantus: Are they not Athenians?
Timon: Yes.
Apemantus: Then I repent not.
                                            Shakespeare, TA 1.1.181

Mark'd ye his words? He would not take the crown.
Therefore 'tis certain he was no ambitious.
                                                        JC 3.2.112

Less common, but in some ways more interesting, are cases where whole clauses have been omitted which are not logically implied: **anapodoton**. When God in the Book of Judges tells the cowardly Gideon to attack the Midianites, Gideon asks for a "sign that thou talkest with me." Gideon knows perfectly well he is being talked to, but he wants a sign that will assure him he is talking with God. This is obvious from the context.

So too when Jefferson writes: "That to secure rights, Governments are instituted among Men, deriving their just powers from the governed," it is obvious from what he has already written that he intends us to supply "We hold self-evident..." So too it is obvious what the assumed concluding clause is for Caligula's "Would that the Roman people had a single neck"—obvious at least to anyone who knows anything about Caligula's character. And experience in the world makes obvious what Estienne meant when he sadly mused, "If youth knew, if age could."

We have gradually moved from smaller, less important omissions to larger, more daring ones. It might seem that the clause is the largest unit which could be intelligibly omitted. That, however, underestimates the resourcefulness with which language is employed. We all know that sometimes we become literally choked with emotion, and are thereby rendered speechless—or at least unable to continue in the direction we set out. I am sure that psychology or physiology has a name for this when it occurs involuntarily. Rhetoric has one for when it is freely used for effect: **aposiopesis**.

And the Lord God said, Behold, the man is become as one of us, to know good and evil: and now, lest he put forth his hand, and take also of the tree of life, and eat, and live forever: Therefore the Lord God sent him forth from the garden of Eden, to till the ground from whence he was taken.

Gen. 3.22

And Moses returned unto the Lord, and said, Oh, this people have sinned a great sin, and have made them gods of

gold. Yet now, if thou wilt forgive their sin—; and if not, blot
me, I pray thee, out of thy book which thou hast written.
                                                          Exod. 32:31

   If thou hadst known, even thou, at least in this thy day, the
things which belong unto thy peace! but now they are hid
from thine eyes.   Luke 19.42

   But meanwhile Neptune saw the ocean's waving commo-
tion....and he summoned the winds by name. "What arrogance
is this, what pride of birth, you winds to meddle here without
my sanction, raising all this trouble? I'll—No the waves come
first! but listen to me. You are going to pay for this!"
                                                              Virgil

Your owne deare sake forst me at first to leave
My Fathers kingdome, There she stopt with teares;
Her swollen hart her speach seemd to bereave.
                                                             Spenser

   For if the sun breed maggots in a dead dog, being a god
kissing carrion—Have you a daughter?
                                      Shakespeare, Ham. 2.2.181

I will have revenges on you both
That all the world shall—I will do such things—
What they are yet, I know not; but they shall be
The terrors of the earth!
                                                       KL 2.4.274

   You could only end just where you begun; that is, to tax
where no revenue is to be found, to—my voice fails me; my
inclination indeed carries me no farther—all is confusion
beyond it.   E. Burke

He catches her in his arms. The fire surrounds them
while—I cannot go on.   Steele

   "You are fond of spectacles," exclaims the stern Tertullian,
"expect the greatest of all spectacles, the last and eternal
judgment of the universe. How shall I admire, how laugh, how
rejoice, how exult, when I behold so many proud monarchs,
and fancied gods, groaning in the lowest abyss of darkness; so
many magistrates, who persecuted the name of the Lord,
liquefying in fiercer fires than they ever kindled against the

Christians;...so many tragedians, more tuneful in the expression of their own sufferings; so many dancers—" But the
humanity of the reader will permit me to draw a veil over the
rest of this infernal description, which the zealous African
pursues in a long variety of affected and unfeeling witticisms.

Gibbon

An aposiopesis does not always have to be used for the
expressing of deep emotion. Sometimes it can be used to
convey casualness, spontaneity. Why, I remember another
time I was with my journalist friend; we had just—but there's
no point in belaboring the matter; you see what I am saying.

Perhaps you think that with the aposiopesis we have
finally reached the furthest extent of possible omission.
Beyond that is simple silence. But, of course, there are few
things about which more has been said and written than the
ineffable. As one contemporary leader of consciousness
raising put it, "To relate the experience to time and place is to
falsify it....There were no words attached to it, no emotions or
feelings, no attitudes, no bodily sensations." To talk about not
being able to talk or decide about something is an **aporia**—and
I don't have words to tell you how often it is used. (De Sade on
his heroine Justine: "A virginal air, large blue eyes very soulful
and appealing, a dazzling fair skin, a supple and resilient body,
a touching voice, teeth of ivory and the loveliest blond hair,
there you have a sketch of this charming creature whose naive
graces and delicate traits are beyond our power to describe.")

Beyond aporia *is* simple silence. The refusal to speak at
all. Where all words are omitted in order to express con-
tentment, or contempt, or catatonia. **Praecisio** is a figure for
which it is understandably difficult to find many examples.
John Cage has actually presented a composition for the piano
during which no sound is to be made. Ramsey Clark, former
Attorney General of the United States, once successfully
defended a group of demonstrators by resting his case before
he ever opened it; the prosecution, his silence seemed to be
saying, had presented nothing that merited a reply. The
philosopher Arthur Schopenhauer, who thought we all would
have been better off if we had never lived, concluded his

idiosyncratic treatise on rhetoric with the proverb: "A chief fruit on the tree of wisdom is silence." Towards this wisdom, this eloquent silence, Samuel Beckett in his life as an author seems to be striving but never quite reaching. As Ralph Waldo Emerson once wrote (in which of his many books I cannot remember), "Good as is discourse, silence is better and shames it."

IV

Man Bites Dog

MY FAVORITE FIGURE of arrangement is the tmesis. Like most of my favorite figures, this one has little practical use—beyond, that is, showing how, once we begin to figure speech, nothing is safe. In **tmesis** we break a work in two, usually to put another word between the parts. (In English only the compounds of "ever" readily lend themselves to tmesis.)

> Which way soever man refer to it   Milton

> How long soever it hath continued, if it be against reason, it is of no force in law.   Coke

> Want to be sure of his spelling. Proof fever. Martin Cunningham forgot to give us his spellingbee conundrum this morning. It is amusing to view the unpar one are alleled embarra two ars is it? double ess ment of a harassed pedlar while gauging au the symmetry of a peeled pear under a cemetery wall. Silly, isn't it?
>   Joyce

> In two words, im possible.   Goldwyn

Examples such as these should put to rest any remaining grammatical scruples we might have about "splitting" an infinitive with an adverb, to say nothing of ending a sentence with a preposition. If an individual word can be guillotined for a good cause, then surely not even the most tightly unified phrase is safe. Of course, in most cases infinitives should not be split, and a preposition should usually be immediately followed by its object. Nonetheless, tmesis reminds us (if we need to be)

39

that in such grammatical matters—never say never. Or, as Winston Churchill is supposed to have replied to someone jokingly critical of him for having ended a sentence with a preposition, "This is the sort of English up with which I will not put."

The general figure on which Churchill's good bad sentence depends is the **hyperbaton**, the name given to any intended deviation from ordinary word order. Churchill himself deviated in order to make fun of people who deviate in the service of grammatical prissiness. But, of course, there are far more reasons for such deviation than that.

Against an elder receive not an accusation, but before two or three witnesses. Them that sin rebuke before all, that others also may fear.   1 Tim. 5:19

Whom God wishes to destroy, he first makes mad.
                                                     Euripides

Arms and the man I sing.   Virgil

Few and signally blest are those whom Jupiter has destined to be cabbage planters.   Rabelais

The gods sent not Corn for the rich men only.
                              Shakespeare, Cor. 1.1.213

Some rise by sin, and some by virtue fall.
                                            MM 2.1.38

Constant you are,
But yet a woman.   1 H IV 2.3.113

Yet I'll not shed her blood,
Nor scar that whiter skin of hers than snow.
                                               O 5.2.3

From such crooked wood as that which man is made of, nothing straight can be fashioned.   Kant

pity this busy monster manunkind not

                                              Cummings

I was in my life alone. Frost

The arms of the morning are beautiful, and the sea
Saint John Perse

About suffering they were never wrong,
The old masters.

Auden

Most frequently a word or phrase is emphasized by placing it either at the beginning or at the end of a sentence or clause. Nevertheless, the mere act of displacing a word or phrase calls attention to it. Shakespeare, for instance, often places an adjective next to a noun other than the one it most appropriately modifies. Sometimes the noun it does appropriately modify is nowhere to be found, and the adjective, usually a weak word, gains considerable power by being a stranger in a strange land. This practice, poetic as it can be, does not lack analogies in our ordinary speech. For instance, we might say that we have spent a restless night when we mean that *we* have spent the night restless.

Keep back thy servant also from presumptuous sins; let them not have dominion over me.
Ps. 19:13

The queen was preparing frenzied ruins for the Roman Capitol. Horace

Ah! when will this long weary day have end,
And lend me leave to come unto my love?

Spenser

What outcries call me from my naked bed?

Kyd

Alas, what ignorant sin have I commited?
Shakespeare, O 4.2.70

Forgive my fearful sails! A&C 3.11.55

Cursing, swearing, reviling, and the like do not signify as speech but as the actions of a tongue accustomed.
Hobbes

The murmurous haunt of flies on summer eves

Keats

Useful it is to distinguish between the hyperbaton and the anastrophe, however rarely done. To simply misplace an adjective is **hyperbaton**; to reverse the order of an adjective and its noun is an **anastrophe**.

Figures pedantical

Shakespeare, LLL 5.2.407

"The retort courteous."..."the quip modest."..."the reply churlish."..."the reproof valiant"..."the countercheck quarrelsome."..."the lie circumstantial," and "the lie direct."

AYLI 5.4.75

How many ages hence
Shall this our lofty scene be acted o'er
In states unborn and accents yet unknown!

JC 3.1.111

Are you good men and true?   MAAN 3.3.1

Military glory pure and simple withers in time into mere recognition by specialists and military historians.

Burckhardt

The poet gives us his essence, but prose takes the mould of the body and mind entire.   Woolf

The old bear...not even a mortal but an anachronism indomitable and invincible out of an old dead time.

Faulkner

Time present and time past
Are both perhaps present in time future,
And time future contained in time past.

Eliot

In other words, to consider a figurative rearrangement as a hyperbaton is to emphasize the displacement of a single element; to consider it as an anastrophe emphasizes the reversal of two elements. The distinction between these two figures is mostly a matter of emphasis, but this emphasis seems

important when we have to deal with the more extreme forms
of figurative arrangement, such as the following kind of
anastrophe.

> Let us die, and rush into the heart of the fight.   Virgil

> Naught, naught, all naught. I can behold no longer
> Th'Antoniad, the Egyptian admiral,
> With all their sixty, fly and turn the rudder.
>
> Shakespeare, A&C 3.10.1

Both of the above are examples of the anastrophe,
hysteron-proteron. This is the stylistic decision to put the cart
before the horse in order to make him push it. In each of these
the biblical commandment has been obeyed—the first has
literally been made last.

An even more extreme anastrophe is the **hypallage** in
which the reversed elements are not grammatically parallel.
When in 2 Samuel 12:27 it is written that the "city of waters" is
taken, we know from the context that this is not literally true.
The city would fall later; all that had been taken here was the
water supply, "the waters of the city." This hypallage, once
recognized, suggests all sorts of meanings the literal statement
would not. As soon as the water supply is taken, the fall of the
city is a foregone conclusion. And in the face of Divine Omni-
potence, even a city as powerful and prosperous as this one,
with its immense fortifications and careful siege precautions, is
a city with foundations of water.

> Who is it that has tied my son to that sword?
>
> Cicero

> The smell has brought the wellknown breezes.
>
> Virgil

> Our gayness and our gift are besmirched
> With rainy marching in the painful field
>
> Shakespeare, H V 4.3.110

> Once upon a tree
> I came across a time   Roethke

More than a little obvious are the risks of such a figure, both for the author who employs it and the reader who thinks he has found one. In fact, I am myself not entirely certain that all the above examples will resist simpler readings. (Indeed, I included one example which I think is wrong—just for fun.)

Usually anastrophes are not such dramatic affairs as the hypallage, in which the very intelligibility of a sentence is risked for the sake of a suggestive phrase. In the more ordinary cases, however, the reversal is so slight that it could be just as easily treated as a hyperbaton. Nonetheless, empahsizing the reversal does have this advantage. While the hyperbaton usually focuses our attention on *where* the displaced element has been moved (to the beginning, to the end?), the anastrophe focuses our attention on *what* has been reversed. Equally common as the reversal of the noun and the adjective is the reversal of the verb with its related nouns or adjectives.

> So God created man in his own image, in the image of God created he him; male and female created he them.
>
> Gen. 1:27

> To each man according to his dream he did interpret. And it came to pass, as he interpreted to us, so it was; me he restored unto mine office, and him he hanged.
>
> Gen. 41:12

> For if he like a madman lived,
> At least he like a wise one died.
>
> Cervantes

> You may my glories and my state depose,
> But not my griefs; still am I king of those.
>
> Shakespeare, R II 4.1.192

> We ready are to try our fortunes
> To the last man.
>
> 2 H IV 4.2.43

> Open-eyed conspiracy
> His time doth take.
>
> Tem. 2.1.309

Wherever fountain or fresh current flowed
Against the eastern ray, translucent, pure
With touch ethereal of heaven's fiery rod
I drank   Milton

"In dreams begins responsibility," wrote Yeats, when most of us would have begun with responsibility and ended in dreams. "Before born babe," Joyce wrote to arrest our attention, "bliss had." And Dickens was just having plain fun with, "Morley was dead, to begin with." We can begin with death and end to begin with. In fact, we can use almost any arrangement we have the will to strength.

And this is true not only of arrangments within an individual sentence, but between different sentences. We can even place one sentence within another. This figure, a tmesis at the sentence level, shares its name with the punctuation mark that often signals it, **parenthesis**.

And it came to pass after all thy wickedness, (woe, woe unto thee! saith the Lord God,) That thou hast also built unto thee an eminent place, and hast made thee a high place in every street.

Ez. 16.23

And in those days Peter stood up in the midst of the disciples and said, (the number of names together were about a hundred and twenty,) Men and brethren, this Scripture must needs have been fulfilled.

Acts 1:15

Wherefore if ye be dead with Christ from the rudiments of the world, why, as though living in the world, are ye subject to ordinances, (Touch not; taste not; handle not; Which all are to perish with the using;) after the commandments and doctrines of men?   Col. 2:20

In Rome you long for the country; in the country—oh inconstant!—you raise the distant city to the stars.

Horace

Next Mettus the swift cars asunder tore,
(Better, false Alban, hadst thou kept thy troth!)
And Tullus dragged the traitor's mingled limbs.

Virgil

I love thilke lasse, (alas why does I love?)
And am forlorne, (alas why am I lorne?)

Spenser

Ha' not you seen, Camillo
(But that's past doubt; you have, or your eye-glass
Is thicker than a cuckold's horn), or heard
(For to a vision so apparent rumour
Cannot be mute) or thought (for cogitation
Resides not in that man does not think)
My wife is slippery?

Shakespeare, WT 1.2.267

Upon a time—unhappy was the clock
That struck the hour!—it was in Rome—accursed
The mansion where!—'twas a feast—O would
Our viands have been poisoned, or at least
Those which I heaved to head!—the good Postumas
What should I say? He was too good to be
Where ill men were.

Cym. 5.5.153

To bring in—God shield us!—a lion among ladies, is a most
dreadful thing.

MND 3.1.32

Why she, even she—
O heaven! a beast, that wants discourse of reason,
Would have mourn'd longer—married with my uncle,
My father's brother.

Ham. 1.2.149

Poetry and Religion (and it is really worth knowing) are "a
product of the smaller intestines."

Carlyle

Nothing is easier than to admit in words the truth of the
universal struggle for life, or more difficult—at least I have
found it so—than constantly to bear this conclusion in mind.

Darwin

The parenthesis can show the author being so overcome
with emotion that he must express it before finishing a
sentence. Or it can show him so at ease, even casual, that he can
mutter an aside *sotto voce.*

A parenthesis can be of any length. In *Genesis,* for instance, the story of Joseph is left for a whole chapter so that the story of Tamar can be told; any adequate interpretation of the Joseph story must explain the function of this parenthetical chapter.

A parenthesis which is too long we criticize as a digression. But not even digressions are all bad. Many a great comic work of fiction is carried by its digressions, much as many comic dramas are carried by the rascally minor characters. Read Lawrence Sterne's *Tristram Shandy.* It does for the digression what *Finnegans Wake* does for the misspelling. There is even, in the midst of one of the many digressions, a chapter entitled "A Digression on Digressions." However, even in this metadigression, Sterne couldn't stick to the point.

V

Reds in the Red

WHAT THIS TITLE means depends upon how we interpret "red" and "reds." The interpretations that come most readily to mind are probably those in which at least one of these words is taken as a substitute for an associated word. "In the red" frequently means financial loss, the color of the ink used to record the loss being used to indicate the loss itself. Then again, red is also associated with blood; and so through ferocious battles rivers of red routinely flow. Red is the color of the Russian flag, and hence a country can endure a red scare, or be subverted by reds. Red is a distinctive human hair color, and those who have it are often known by it. It is also the distinctive pigment in the plumage of Rhode Island chickens and Cincinnati baseball players. And when we get very angry, it is all that we see. On the other hand, we sometimes see nothing clearly after eating a bowl of red, on account of the tears the chili provokes. This string of reds could be continued indefinitely. Once you start substituting, it is hard to know where to stop. But we should probably stop before we see red sails in the sunset or scarlet women in the pink.

From this indefinite catalogue we can turn with relief to the concrete pragmatism of Joe Jacobs' "We wa. robbed!" With little risk of being misunderstood, but with much risk of being thought illiterate, we can always substitute one grammatical form for another: **enallage**.

But see where Somerset and Clarence comes!
Shakespeare, 3 H VI 4.2.3

49

Is there not wars? Is there not employment?

2 H IV 1.2.85

The posture of your blows are yet unknown

JC 5.1.33

To show an unfelt sorrow is an office
Which the false man does easy.   M 2.3.143

I takes my man Friday with me.   Defoe

Curiouser and curiouser   Carroll

There are more possibilities here than might at first be obvious. Historians (and characters from Damon Runyon) regularly substitute the present tense for the past, to vivify that past. A monarch, or a Las Vegas nightclub star will ordinarily refer to himself as "we," without anyone suspecting schizophrenia. To quote Queen Victoria, "We are not amused."

Nonetheless, the most important type of enallage is the substitution of one part of speech for another. This is the **anthimeria** for which the later Shakespeare has a demonstrable penchant. The opportunities here are dizzying. When Shakespeare writes of "this beneath world" we know what he means despite the fact that he has used a preposition for an adjective. We can substitute just about anything for anything else. However, the most important parts of speech are the most commonly substituted for.

The painful warrior famoused for fight

Shakespeare, S 25.9

Such stuff as madmen
Tongue, and brain not   Cym. 5.4.146

The thunder would not peace at my bidding.

KL 4.6.103

Thank me no thankings, nor proud me no prouds.

R&J 5.153

Lord Angelo dukes it well.

MM 3.2.100

Wouldst thou be window'd in great Rome and see
Thy master.   A&C 4.14.72

Taint him with license of ink.
If thou thou'st him some thrice, it shall not be amiss
                                                   TN 3.2.47

These were all substitutions for the verb. The following
are for the noun.

I am going in search of the great perhaps.
                                                   Rabelais

The fair, the chaste, and unexpressive she.
                                    Shakespeare, AYLI 3.3.10

Goodness, growing to a plurisy,
Dies in his own too-much.   Ham. 4.7.118

The mutable, rank-scented many
                                                   T&C 3.1.65

Every why hath a wherefore.
                                                   CE 2.2.45

The hot of him is purest in the heart.
                                                   Stevens

O dark dark dark. They all go into the dark.
The vacant interstellar spaces, the vacant into the vacant.
                                                   Eliot

he sang his didn't he danced his did.
                                                   Cummings

There are two particular forms of substituting a noun for
an adjective that deserve special attention. One is our old
friend hendiadys, about which we need say no more. The
other, for which the name **antiptosis** has been suggested, is
similar to a hendiadys. Instead of adding an "and" between the
old and new nouns, an antiptosis adds an "of." The glorious
kingdom becomes not the kingdom and the glory but the
kingdom of glory.

Why are thou so far from helping me, and from the words of
my roaring?

Ps. 22:1

And above all these things put on charity, which is the
bond of perfectness.

Col. 1:17

The King's name is a tower of strength.

Shakespeare, R III 5.3.12

Although from one perspective anthimeria might seem
to undermine grammatical categories, from another it depends
upon them for its figurative effects. The anthimeria, to be an
anthimeria, needs a stable grammatical structure to rebel
against. Only a theist can be a sinner.

On the other and, all figurative substitutions do not sin
against the great god Grammar. In fact, the most common
substitutions do not. A word will be substituted for another of
identical grammatical form and related meaning. Usually the
relationship is between the nouns and is a fairly obvious
one—cause and effect, the container and contained, raw
material and finished object. To substitute the contained for
the container, the effect for the cause, is called **metonymy.**

And the Lord said unto her, Two nations are in thy womb.

Gen. 25:23

At the mouth of two witnesses, or three witnesses, shall he
that is worthy of death be put to death.

Deut. 17:6

He gave also their increase unto the caterpillar, and their
labor unto the locust.

Ps. 78:46

And I also have given you cleanness of teeth in all your
cities, and want of bread in all your places

Amos 4:6

I turned to see the voice that spake with me.

Rev. 1:12

Rome has spoken; the case is concluded.

Augustine

He tilts with piercing steel at bold Mercutio's breast.
Shakespeare, R&J 3.1.163

Is it not strange that sheep's guts should hale souls out of men's bodies?

MAAN 2.3.61

I must comfort the weaker vessel, as doublet and hose ought to show itself courageous to petticoat.

AYLI 2.4.6

Bell, book, and candle shall not drive me back.

KJ 3.3.12

Amazement seized
The rebel thrones.   Milton

As learned Commentators view
In Homer more than Homer knew

Swift

The pen is mightier than the sword.

Bulwer-Lytton

Her voice is full of money.

Fitzgerald

These are the commonest form of the metonymy.

Sometimes the substitutions are not immediately clear. When in the above passage Amos prophesies that God in His wrath is going to give the Hebrews clean teeth, we know this has nothing to do with dental hygiene. But it is only on reflection that we realize that you don't have to brush your teeth if you don't eat. Amos was predicting a famine.

At times the connection between two nouns in a metonymy might seem so remote that we are inclined to think that a double substitution has occurred, a metonymic two-step. For instance, in *Genesis* it is written "they came under the shadow of my roof." Roof stands for house, but house stands for protection. Such a double metonymy is called a **metalepsis**. So Paul will speak of "preaching the cross," the cross being the instrument of crucifixion and the crucifixion of Jesus being the cause of the redemption—Paul was preaching redemption. So too in *Measure for Measure* Shakespeare has a character say "My father's grave/Did utter forth a voice." It was not the grave, nor the body within the grave, but something that was once within the body that did the uttering.

These are the best examples of metalepses, along with Virgil's "some beards of corn" (beard for silk, silk for the whole ear). But metalepsis is an inherently problematic figure. More often than not we will be unable to agree whether or not to employ this term at all. Was it really a two-step or just one big hop? Such is the dizzily dancing world of figurative substitution.

This becomes even more evident when a metonymy involves a part of speech other than the usually tame noun. Only occasionally and in well-defined contexts can, for instance, one verb be readily substituted for another. To ask God to judge the wicked is really to ask Him to punish them. And when someone shouts "Thank you!" from one country club tennis court to another, he usually means "Please get my ball," and also, "Every member of this club is polite."

> And also all that generation were gathered unto their fathers: and there arose another generation after them, which knew not the Lord, nor yet the works which He had done for Israel.   Judg. 2:10

> For the Lord knoweth the way of the righteous: but the way of the ungodly shall perish.   Ps. 1:6

> Why do ye not understand my speech? even because ye cannot hear my word.   John 8:42

When the substitution is not of verbs or nouns but of adjectives, the effect can be quite striking.

I do not ask much:
I beg cold comfort.

Shakespeare, KJ 5.7.41

A man that studies revenge keeps his own wounds green.

Bacon

Her who still weeps with spungie eyes.

Donne

Blind mouths

Milton

This dark brightness that falls from the stars.

Corneille

And that White Sustenance - Despair.

Dickinson

The Cold War.

Baruch

These are examples of the most problematic of metonymies, the **catachresis**. The equivalent Latin term, **abusio**, suggests the tone of many attempts to define it. In using a catachresis—by describing a mouth as blind, for instance—a writer seems to have come close to abusing the legitimate function of substitution. He has made a substitution of a word which, far from having an easily definable connection with the substitutee, seems to have been chosen precisely because of its inappropriateness. Although this happens most frequently with adjectives, the term catachresis can also be applied to a substitution of a noun or verb that similarly jars our sensibilities.

Ye have made our savour to be abhorred in the eyes of Pharaoh.

Exod. 5:21

O God, why hast thou cast us off for ever? Why doth thine anger smoke against the sheep of thy pasture?

Ps. 74:1

The very pink of courtesy.   Cervantes

But ah, who can deceive his destiny?...So fickle be the
termes of mortall state.   Spenser

His complexion is perfect gallows.

Shakespeare, Tem. 1.1.33

You tread upon my patience.   H IV 1.1.433

Methinks my favour here begins to warp

WT 1.2.365

A man may see how this world goes with no eyes. Look
with thine ears: see how yond justice rails upon yon simple
thief.   KL 4.6.154

The Oriel Common Room stank of logic.

Newman

I shall not live in vain
If I can ease one Life the Aching
Or cool one Pain.

Dickinson

the voice of your eyes is deeper than all roses

cummings

Those who do regard catachresis as an abuse will usually
try to clear the Bible and Shakespeare from the charge of ever
having taken such an illicit turn. Others will respond that the
highest function of language is to reveal to us indefinable
connections, those moments when we understand but know
not why.

On this matter I feign no hypothesis, but rather turn with
relief to the least problematic, and most useful, of all
metonymies, the **synecdoche**. Here the connection is that of a
part and a whole, a genus and a species.

And Abram took Sarai his wife, and...the souls they had
gotten in Haran and they went forth to go into the land of
Canaan   Gen. 12:5

For dust thou art, and unto dust shalt thou return.

Gen. 3:19

And I am come down to deliver them out of the hand of the Egyptians, and to bring them up out of that land unto a good land and a large, unto a land flowing with milk and honey.

Exod. 3:8

Through thee will we push down our enemies: through thy name will we tread them under that rise up against us. For I will not trust in my bow, neither shall my sword save me.

Ps. 44:5

Then Judas, which had betrayed him, when he saw that he was condemned, repented himself, and brought again the thirty pieces of silver to the chief priests and elders, Saying, I have sinned in that I have betrayed the innocent blood.

Matt. 27:3

Now I beseech you, brethren, mark them which cause divisions and offenses contrary to the doctrine which ye have learned; and avoid them. For they that are such serve not our Lord Jesus Christ, but their own belly; and by good words and fair speeches deceive the hearts of the simple.

Rom. 16:17

Paris is well worth a Mass.   Henri IV

Was this the face that launched a thousand ships,
And burnt the topless towers of Ilium?

Marlowe

These are the ushers of Marcius. Before him he carries noise.

Shakespeare, Cor. 2.1.174

Yet, poor old heart, he holp the heavens to rain.

KL 3.7.62

Pour down thy weather.

KJ 4.2.109

I saw them in the war
Like to a pair of lions smear'd with prey.

TNK 1.4.17

Take thy face hence.

                                                    M 5.3

The man i' th' moon's too slow—till new-born chins
Be rough and razorable.

                                                    T 2.1.293

There was never yet fair woman but she made mouths in a
glass.

                                                    KL 3.2.35

And never, since the middle summer's spring,
Met we on hill, in dale, forest, or mead...
To dance our ringlets to the whistling wind.

                                                    MND 2.1.82

A hungry stomach has no ears.   La Fontaine

The broken wall, the burning roof and tower
And Agamemnon dead   Yeats

I should have been a pair of ragged claws
Scuttling across the floor of silent seas.

                                                    Eliot

As these examples suggest, the substitution of a part for
a whole is the most common synecdoche. But its commonness
does not preserve us from the dizzying swirl that begins to
surround us the moment we start the process of substitution.
People who would dismiss catachresis with a shrug will still ask
plaintively if synecdochic relationships really exist outside of
language. Perhaps Blake was right and the whole world *is*
contained within a grain of sand; perhaps he was even right
when he wrote that "The Atoms of Democritus/ And Newton's
Particles of light/ Are but sands upon the Red sea shore/ Where
Israel's tents do shine so bright." Perhaps given persons or
peoples, given places or times, are tabernacles for greater
wholes. These ineffably real synecdoches, if such there be, are
properly called symbols.

Many writers energetically spend their lives searching for
the symbolic. Some think that on occasion they find it. Others
never can quite make up their minds. (These we call surrealists.)

And still others conclude their search in the spirit so aptly expressed by the immortal Joe Jacobs: "I should of stood in bed."

VI

More Than Enough

THE MOST INFLUENTIAL work written in early modern Europe on the figures of speech was *De Copia* by Erasmus. As the title suggests, Erasmus was primarily interested in teaching how to write more copiously. His readers would learn how to use many words where the common herd used only a few. At one point he developed more than a hundred variations on the sentence "Your letter has delighted me very much." "With what joy do you suppose I am filled when I recognize your soul in your letter! When the letter carrier handed me your letter, my spirit at once began to thrill with an ineffable joy. How shall I tell you what joy titillated the spirit of your Erasmus when he received your letter?" Hemingway would not approve.

The baroque identification of eloquence with copiousness is so far from official twentieth century taste that scarcely a guidebook on writing does not contain an admonition such as the following: "Be brief. Do not repeat yourself. Say what you have to say in as few words as possible. To belabor your point is to risk boring your reader—or even insulting his intelligence."

Erasmus would not lack words for a reply. He would point out that the author of this advice had thought it so important that he was not brief, did repeat himself, used as many words as he dared, and had insulted the intelligence of his reader by contradicting himself in the process. "How shall I tell what joy titillated the spirit of your Erasmus when he read your foolish passage?"

The simplest form of copiousness is **pleonasm**. We know we have a pleonasm when we can eliminate words without

61

changing meanings. Pleonasms are what blue pencils remove. But blue pencils are not always right—or at least not always on the side of God. The Bible is full of pleonasms. As often as not, words like "face," "mouth," "sons," "children," "name," "hand," "voice," are used pleonastically—and certain formulaic phrases like "it came to pass" always are.

> And the Spirit of God moved upon the face of the waters.
> Gen. 1:2

> And they heard the voice of the Lord God walking in the garden in the cool of the day.
> Gen. 3:8

> By reason of the voice of my groaning my bones cleave to my skin.   Ps. 102:5

> At her feet he bowed, he fell, he lay down: at her feet he bowed, he fell: where he bowed, there he fell down dead.
> Judg. 5:27

> The conclave of all the night's stars, those potentates blazing in the heavens that bring winter and summer to mortal men, the constellations   Aeschylus

> A child of our grandmother Eve, a female; or, for thy more sweet understanding, a woman.
> Shakespeare, LLL 1.1.263

> The inaudible and noiseless foot of time
> AW 5.3.41

> When that I was and a little tiny boy
> TN 5.1.398

> I saw the wound, I saw it with mine eyes.
> R&J 3.2.52

> This was the most unkindest cut of all.
> Shakespeare, JC 3.2.188

Give you a reason on compulsion! if reasons were as plenty as blackberries, I would give no man a reason upon compulsion, I.

1 H IV 2.4.267

I have discovered that all human evil comes from this, man's being unable to sit still in a room.

Pascal

Drinking when we are not thirsty and making love at all seasons, Madam: That is all there is to distinguish us from the other Animals. Beaumarchais

I saw a woman flayed the other day. And you would be surprised at the difference it made in her appearance for the worse. Swift

"This" in the Pascal quote and "that" in the Beaumarchais are inserted to draw attention to what follows. Such a pleonasm is sometimes given the more specific name **asterismos**. Some writers will italicize a phrase in order to emphasize it, others will simply put an asterismos in front of it. The most frequent asterismos in the Bible is "behold," while that in contemporary sports interviews is "hey." "Behold, the Lord God said...," and "Hey, that game was..."

Asterismoses aside, I would not be surprised if you balked at my treatment of at least a few of those passages as pleonasms; and I will bet they were the passages you liked the best. A pleonasm which works very well seems to be bent on transcending itself. In fact, I am not comfortable with the very first example. I cannot quite read "face" as simply a pleonasm. It is a substitution for "surface" that makes the scene imaginable for me, a divine wind wrinkling the waves.

This example is useful in pointing to the close connection that exists between figures of addition and those of substitution. Sometimes what starts as a pleonasm can become a substitution. This process is clearest with the use of epithets. A king might be called Eric the Red, or Richard the Lion Hearted, or (my favorite) Ethelred the Unready. In time everyone would know who was meant by The Red or The Lion Hearted (and would have known who was The Unready if he had lasted long enough).

And so too God Our Heavenly Father can become our Heavenly Father, or simply Our Father. Jesus the Christ can become Christ the Lord which in turn can be shortened to The Lord. Thus Christians address "Our Father" in "The Lord's Prayer."

We can in fact use substitution to achieve the characteristic effects of addition. This happens when we substitute more words for less. This figure, **periphrasis**, differs from pleonasm in that we need more than a blue pencil to retrieve the literal meaning.

We are all too familiar with this particular mode. We live in a world in which the killing of a spy is the elimination with extreme prejudice of an intelligence-gathering operative. And in this world we secretly think that if all periphrasis could be eliminated, bureaucracy would wither away, along with its academic handmaidens, the social sciences. We need to be reminded, therefore, that legitimate uses of periphrasis do exist (such as substituting "academic handmaidens of bureaucracy" for "social sciences" in order to contribute to their elimination with extreme prejudice).

And thou shalt go to thy fathers in peace; thou shalt be buried in a good old age.   Gen. 15:15

And he said, Who art thou? And she answered, I am Ruth thine handmaid: spread therefore thy skirt over thine handmaid; for thou art a near kinsman.

Ruth 3:9

Yea, I think it meet, as long as I am in this tabernacle, to stir you up by putting you in rememberance; Knowing that shortly I must put off this my tabernacle, even as our Lord Jesus Christ hath showed me.

2 Pet. 1:13

Now he is traveling the dark road to the place from which they say no one has ever returned.   Catullus

To meet the demands of nature   Sallust

From pro's and con's they fell to a warmer way of
disputing.   Cervantes

The moist star
Upon whose influence Neptune's empire stands
                           Shakespeare Ham. 1.1.118

While memory holds a seat
In this distracted globe   Ham. 1.4.96

Your daughter and the Moor are now making the beast
with two backs.   O 1.1.117

Night's candles are burnt out.   R&J 3.5.9

When that fell arrest
Without all bail shall carry me away.
                           Shakespeare, S 74.1

I hope you do not think me prone to an iteration of nuptials.
                                            Congreve

Cunegonde...saw Dr. Pangloss behind some bushes giving
a lesson in experimental philosophy to her mother's waiting-
woman, a little brunette who seemed eminently teachable.
                                            Voltaire

The author of our Hemingway writing handbook was
using pleonasm on a far larger scale than the phrase. He gave
us a series of sentences in which each said essentially the same
thing in different words. The Latin word for this is undoubtedly
the most sensible: **accumulatio**. I, however, must admit an
attraction for its competitor, **congeries**, which suggests to me a
writhing mass of intertwined eels.

Hear, O Israel, ye approach this day unto battle against
your enemies: let not your hearts faint, fear not, and do not
tremble, neither be ye terrified because of them; For the Lord
your God is he that goeth with you, to fight for you against
your enemies, to save you.
                                            Deut. 20:3

Give ear to my words, O Lord; consider my meditation.
Hearken unto the voice of my cry, my King, and my God: for
unto thee will I pray.
My voice shalt thou hear in the morning, O Lord; in the
morning will I direct my prayer unto thee, and will look up.
Ps. 5:1

We have heard the pride of Moab, (he is exceeding proud,)
his loftiness, and his arrogancy, and his pride, and the
haughtiness of his heart.
Jer. 48:29

All is flux, nothing stays still.   Heraclitus

He departed, he went hence; he burst forth, he was gone.
Cicero

I say again that this is most true, and all history bears
witness to it, that men may second Fortune, but they cannot
thwart her—they may weave her web, but they cannot break
it.   Machiavelli

I will not excuse you; you shall not be excus'd; excuses shall
not be admitted; there is no excuse shall serve you; you shall
not be excus'd.   Shakespeare, 2 H IV 5.1.5

But now I am cabin'd, cribb'd, confin'd, bound in
To saucy doubts and fears.
Mac. 3.4.24

I take thy hand—this hand,
As soft as dove's down and as white as it,
Or Ethiopians's tooth, or the fann'd snow that's bolted
By th' northern blasts twice o'er.
WT 4.4.355

Where is your ancient courage? You were us'd
To say extremity was the trier of spirits;
That common chances common men could bear;
That when the sea was calm, all boats alike
Show'd mastership in floating; fortunes's blows
When most struck home, being gentle wounded craves
A noble cunning.
Cor. 4.1.1.

You must either conquer and rule or serve and lose, suffer or triumph, be the anvil or the hammer.

Goethe

Man cannot afford to be a naturalist, to look at nature directly, but only with the side of his eye. He must look through her and beyond her. To look at her is as fatal as to look at the head of Medusa. It turns the man of science to stone.

Thoreau

A common technique of accumulation is the simple **antithesis**. Rather than saying something and then repeating it in other words, you both deny its contrary and assert it. The basic effect is the same; you have said the thing in two different ways. Nonetheless, the antithesis does have the advantage of giving a sense of completeness with only two items. In the ordinary accumulatio it is difficult to avoid the feeling that the number of repetitions was arbitrary. (How many eels does it take to make a proper congeries?)

Do ye thus requite the Lord, O foolish people and unwise?

Deut. 32:6

Now the Egyptians are men, and not God; and their horses flesh, and not spirit. When the Lord shall stretch out his hand, both he that helpeth shall fall, and he that is holpen shall fall down, and they shall all fall together.

Isa. 31:3

Shall not the day of the Lord be darkness, and not light? even very dark, and no brightness in it?

Amos 5:20

All things were made by Him, and without Him was not anything made that was made.

John 1:3

Think not that I am come to send peace on earth: I came not to send peace, but the sword.

Matt. 10:34

The greatest crimes are caused by surfeit, not by want. Men do not become tyrants so as not to suffer cold.

Aristotle

This law then, gentlemen, was not written, but born. It is a law which we have not learned, received from others or read, but which we have derived, absorbed and copied from nature itself.   Cicero

Necessity compels me, and not pleasure.

                                                                    Dante

I speak not out of weak surmises, but from proof as strong as my grief and as certain as I expect my revenge.

                                        Shakespeare, Cym. 3.4.23

Think not the king did banish thee,
But thou the king.

                                                    R II 1.3.279

Let's carve him as a dish fit for the gods,
Not hew him as a carcass fit for hounds.

                                                    JC 2.1.173

A man should be mourned at his birth, not at his death.

                                                    Montesquieu

The natural flights of the human mind are not from pleasure to pleasure, but from hope to hope.

                                                    Dr. Johnson

Insects sting, not in malice, but because they want to live. It is the same with critics; they desire our blood, not our pain.

                                                    Nietzsche

The artist appeals to that part of our being which is not dependent on wisdom: to that in us which is a gift and not an acquisition—and, therefore, more permanently enduring.

                                                    Conrad

Another common technique of accumulation by negation is the **epanorthosis**. Frequently in ordinary talking we say something and then think better of it. Then we correct ourselves by making our statement more accurate or by repenting of it entirely. Both of these kinds of correction can be used for the general effect of an accumulatio, and the particular effect of the antithesis.

These six things doth the Lord hate; yea, seven are an abomination unto him. Prov. 6:16

Behold, the hour cometh, yea, is now come, that ye shall be scattered, every man to his own.

John 16:31

I labored more abundantly than they all: yet not I, but the grace of God which was with me.

1 Cor. 15:10

Religion is a disease, but it is a noble disease.

Heraclitus

Give me chastity, but not yet.

Augustine

Not all men are wise; indeed, very few are.

Guicciardini

So was he overcome, not overcome,
But to her yeelded of his owne accord.

Spenser

A good heart, Kate, is the sun and the moon; or rather, the sun, and not the moon, for it shines bright and never changes, but keeps his course truly.

Shakespeare, H V 5.2.160

Your brother (no, no brother! yet the son—
Yet not the son—I will not call him son
Of him I was about to call his father)
Hath heard your praises,

AYLI 2.3.19

That it should not come to this!
But two months dead!—nay, not so much—not two.

Ham. 1.2.137

He in a few minutes ravished this fair creature, or at least would have ravished her if she had not, by a timely compliance, prevented him. Fielding

To make a prairie it takes clover and one bee,
One clover, and a bee,

and revery.
The revery alone will do,
If bees are few.   Dickinson

When a Forsyte died—but no Forsyte had as yet died;
death being contrary to their principles, they took precautions
against it.   Galsworthy

The epanorthosis became a dominant technique in the
later work of Henry James, as it was useful to convey that
complexity of consciousness which fascinated him. "He would
have, strangely enough, as it might seem to him, to come back
home for it, and there get the impression of her rather
pointedly, or at least all impatiently and independently,
awaiting him." Got that?

Even a reader comfortable with James the Old Pretender
might not feel quite at ease with epanorthosis when it is used in
argument. He might feel that here more was going on than just
accumulation or antithesis, and that he does not quite trust the
more. In this suspicion he would be shrewd.

Suppose I now ostentatiously repented of something I
had earlier written. Suppose I confessed that in comparing
bureaucrats to social scientists I was being unfair to someone.
Shouldn't my reader admire me for having so candidly
admitted my earlier mistake? Perhaps. But he might just ask
me why I did not remove the slander altogether. Wasn't I
intentionally making the mistake in order to correct it? He
might ask that question, and instinctively place his hand on his
wallet.

And he would certainly want to keep his hand there if I
had been using the epanorthosis the way trial lawyers
sometimes use the judge. They make inadmissible statements
which the judge will rule out of order, but only after the jury
has heard them.

It is a small step from this form of epanorthosis to the
praeteritio. Here the lawyer does not even give the judge a
chance to rule him out of order. He gets the inadmissible
evidence before the jury in the process of announcing that he is
not going to introduce it. We use a harmless form of praeteritio

when we introduce material with phrases like "not to mention" or "to say nothing of." These are innocence itself compared to the frequent use of praeteritio in matters of public dispute. If I were to declare any figure inherently disreputable (which, of course, I will not), this would be the one. Neither will I mention that the only American president who repeatedly used the praeteritio was also the only one who had to resign. I will not mention it, despite its obvious relevance to our present discussion, because anything that might be interpreted as a political statement would be entirely inappropriate in a book such as this.

VII

There There

A MOST MEMORABLE description of Oakland, California, was that offered by Gertrude Stein (by way of explaining why she left): "There is no there there." If she had said simply "Nothing of interest ever happens there," her remark would not have been remembered, for people—rightly or wrongly—say that about Oakland all the time.

Unfortunately, Stein's statement can cause us almost as much trouble as it can the Oakland Chamber of Commerce. How does a witticism like hers work? Our immediate response is "By repetition." But how does repetition fit into the system of classification which has served us so well?

We might be tempted to say that repetition is a particular form of addition. For instance, in discussing misspellings of addition we could suggest a further classification (as we did) by asking *what* has been added. We can add either letters that do not already occur in the word or letters that do. If the latter, then we have the peculiar form of addition called repetition. A nice try; but not nice enough.

The problem is that the repetition of letters does not always involve misspelling. I do not have to misspell "misspell" in order to have an impressive repetition of letters. Repetitions, both spelling and otherwise, do not need to be devia_ions from ordinary usage; repetition is a choice in ordinary usage. To try to make it anything else is to let the tail wag the dog, to let the system dictate our perception of the practice. Neither can we exclude such an important group of stylistic figures because it happens to cause difficulties for our definition of "figure." So much the worse for the definition. And for the time being let us

73

not worry about finding a new one. Let's just permit the old one to rest in peace while we learn about the usefulness of repetition.

Stein's quip is a peculiar form of repetition, the repetition of the same word or root with different grammatical functions or forms. This figure, the **polyptoton**, is used frequently in aphorisms, probably because it is rarely recognized as a figure at all and hence the phrase is more likely to be experienced as strikingly original. (Mark Twain found that learning to navigate the Mississippi made the moments of aesthetic submission to the river less frequent, the price anyone pays for mastery over anything.)

Cursed be Canaan; a servant of servants shall he be unto his brethren.   Gen. 9:25

I will wipe Jerusalem as a man wipeth a dish, wiping it, and turning it upside down.   2 Kings 21:13

The treacherous dealers have delt treacherously; yea, the treacherous dealers have dealt very treacherously.
Isa. 24:16

But evil men and seducers shall wax worse and worse, deceiving, and being deceived.   2 Tim. 3:13

When he ascended up on high, he led captivity captive, and gave gifts to men.   Eph. 4:8

Light be the earth upon you, lightly rest.
Euripides

Nothing is enough to the man for whom enough is too little.
Epicurus

He cures most in whom most have faith.
Galen

Who shall stand guard to the guards themselves?
Juvenal

We both exist and know that we exist, and rejoice in this existence and this knowledge.   Augustine

No one can more easily deceive others than someone who is reputed never to deceive.

Guicciardini

He was not born to shame:
Upon his brow shame is asham'd to sit.

Shakespeare, R&J 3.2.91

But when I tell him he hates flatterers,
He says he does, being then most flattered.

JC 2.1.207

Unheedful vows may heedfully be broken.

TGV 2.6.11

So shalt thou feed on Death, that feeds on men,
And Death once dead, there's no more dying then.

S 146.13

Few men speak humbly of humility, chastely of chastity, skeptically of skepticism.

Pascal

The religion most prevalent in our northern colonies is...the dissidence of dissent, and the protestantism of the Protestant religion.

Burke

Let the people think they govern, and they will be governed.

Penn

Man would sooner have the void for his purpose than be void of purpose.

Nietzsche

Mock mockers after that
That would not lift a hand maybe
To help good, wise or great
To bar that foul storm out, for we
Traffic in mockery.

Yeats

Love is an irresistible desire to be irresistibly desired.

Frost

One can also repeat a word in the same (or similar) grammatical form but with a different meaning. This figure, a kind of extended pun, appropriately has a name like a long snake, **antanaclasis**.

Follow me; and let the dead bury their dead.

Matt. 8:22

And when he had given thanks, he brake it, and said, Take, eat; this is my body, which is broken for you.

1 Cor. 11:24

O mortal man, think mortal thoughts!

Euripides

Sits he on never so high a throne, a man still sits on his bottom.

Montaigne

Time, which is the author of authors.

Bacon

It seems to me most strange that men should fear;
Seeing that death, a necessary end,
Will come when it will come.

Shakespeare, JC 2.2.35

I have no other but a woman's reason. I think him so, because I think him so.

TGV 1.2.23

True eloquence takes no heed of eloquence, true morality takes no heed of morality.   Pascal

We must all hang together, or assuredly we shall all hang separately.   Franklin

Experience is only half of experience.

Goethe

That night, that year of now done darkness I wretch lay wrestling with (my God) my God.

Hopkins

The gambling known as business looks with austere disfavor on the business known as gambling.

Bierce

The business of America is business.

                                                    Coolidge

Dead battles, like dead generals, hold the military mind in
their dead grip.   Tuchman

A particular species of antanaclasis is the **ploce**, by
which one moves between a more particular meaning of a
word and a more general one, such as when one uses a
proper name to designate both an individual and then the
general qualities which that person is thought to possess. In
Romans Paul warns, "They are not all Israel, which are of
Israel." James Joyce, in a somewhat different spirit, com-
ments on those who are "more Irish than the Irish." And
Timon the misanthrope is asked in Shakespeare's play
about him, "Is man so hateful to thee/That art thyself a
man?" I probably should not have included ploce as a
separate figure, much too specific by half. But I couldn't
resist it because of the English translation one handbook
suggested: "word folding." I can now no longer come across
a ploce without imagining the word having been separated
from its sentence, beaten stiff like the white of an egg, and
folded back in.

The isolcolon is, in a strange way, the counterpart of the
polyptoton. While the polyptoton repeats the same word in
different grammatical forms, the **isolcolon** repeats the same
grammmatical forms in different words. Moreover, the
polyptoton is a witticism that risks seeming contrived if
extended beyond the sentence; the isolcolon is scarcely
noticeable unless used over whole passages. Its repeatedly
balanced phrases may at times seem stuffy, but rarely
contrived. It is most frequently the port-and-oak-panelled-
study style of an Edward Gibbon, all irony and no passion.
(Although it covers equally well the prize-fighter's boast, "The
bigger they are, the harder they fall.")

But in all things approving ourselves as the ministers of God,
in much patience, in afflictions, in necessities, in distresses. In
stripes, in imprisonments, in tumults, in afflictions, in labors, in
watchings, in fastings; By pureness, by knowledge, by long-
suffering, by kindness, by the Holy Ghost, by love unfeigned,

by the word of truth, by the power of God, by the armor of righteousness on the right hand and on the left. By honor and dishonor, by evil report and good report: as deceivers, and yet true; as unknown, and yet well known; as dying, and, behold, we live; as chastened, and not killed; as sorrowful, yet always rejoicing; as poor, yet making many rich; as having nothing, and yet possessing all things.   2 Cor. 6:4

In peace, sons bury their fathers; in war, fathers bury their sons.   Herodotus

So, when Jove saw the world was one great ocean,
Only one woman left of all those thousands,
And only one man left of all those thousands,
Both innocent and worshipful, he parted
The clouds, turned loose the Northwind, swept them off,
Showed earth to heaven again, and sky to land.
                                                              Ovid

Human Life! Its duration is momentary, its substance in perpetual flux, its senses dim, its physical organism perishable, its consciousness a vortex, its destiny dark, its repute uncertain—in fact, the material element is a rolling stream, the spiritual element dreams and vapor, life a war and a sojourning in a far country, fame oblivion. What can see us through?   Marcus Aurelius

I speak Spanish to God, Italian to women, French to men, and German to my horse.   Charles V

Paris: Beguil'd, divorced, wronged, spited, slain!...
Capulet: Despis'd, distressed, hated, martyr'd, kill'd.
                                       Shakespeare, R&J 4.5.55

If you prick us, do we not bleed? if you tickle us, do we not laugh? if you poison us, do we not die? and if you wrong us, shall we not revenge?   MV 3.1.65

Always the dullness of the fool is the whetstone of the wits.
                                                    AYLI 1.2.59

Your reasons at dinner have been sharp and sententious; pleasant without scurrility, witty without affection, audacious

without impudency, learned without opinion, strange without
heresy.   LLL 5.1.2

See how the World its Veterans rewards!
A Youth of frolicks, an old Age of Cards,
Fair to no purpose, artful to no end,
Young without Lovers, old without a Friend,
A Fop their Passion, but their Prize a Sot,
Alive, ridiculous, and dead, forgot!

Pope

The various modes of worship, which prevailed in the
Roman world, were all considered by the people, as equally
true; by the philosopher, as equally false; and by the
magistrate, as equally useful.   Gibbon

As students of nature we are pantheists, as poets polytheists,
as moral beings monotheists.

Goethe

The world will ever bow to those who hold principle above
policy, truth above diplomacy, and right above consistency.
Macaulay

The louder he talked of his honor, the faster we counted our
spoons.   Emerson

Most repetition is a far simpler kind than any we have
seen so far. Mostly it is the repetition of the same word (or
words) in the same grammatical form with the same meaning.
The general name given to such an elementary repetition
is.....**repetitio**.

Vanity of vanities, saith the preacher, vanity of vanities; all is
vanity.   Eccles. 1:1

And I will sanctify my great name, which was profaned
among the heathen, which ye have profaned in the midst of
them; and the heathen shall know that I am the Lord, saith the
Lord God, when I shall be sanctified in you before their eyes.
Ez. 36:23

I hate and I love. Why I do so, perhaps you ask. I know not,
but I feel it and I am in torment.

Catullus

But jealous souls will not be answer'd so;
They are not ever jealous for the cause,
But jealous for they are jealous

Shakespeare, O 3.4.158

Here come more voices.—
Your voices! For your voices I have fought;
Watch'd for your voices; for your voices bear
Of wounds two dozen odd; battles thrice six
I have seen and heard of; for your voices have
Done many things, some less, some more.
Your Voices!

Cor. 2.3.120

Light seeking light doth light of light beguile.

LLL 1.1.77

And my large kingdom for a little grave,
A little little grave, an obscure grave.

R II 3.3.153

Not, I'll not carrion comfort,
Despair, not feast on thee.

Hopkins

The polysyndeton is an unusual figure of repetition
because it is particularly defined by *what* has been repeated.
More commonly the figures of repetition are defined by where
the repeated elements occur. The strongest emphasis can
usually be achieved by repeating a word or phrase immediately: **epizeuxis**.

And the king was much moved, and went up to the chamber
over the gate, and wept: and as he wept, thus he said, O my son
Absalom! my son, my son, Absalom! would God I had died for
thee, O Absalom, my son, my son!

2 Sam. 18:33

My God, my God, why hast thou forsaken me?

Ps. 22:1

Comfort ye, comfort ye my people, saith your God.

Isa. 40:1

O Jerusalem, Jerusalem, thou that killest the prophets, and stonest them which are sent unto thee.

Matt. 23:37

Ah, how they glide by, Postumus, Postumus,
The years, the swift years!

Horace

I am not he, I am not he thou thinkest.

Dante

O Cressid! O false Cressid! false, false, false!

Shakespeare, T&C 5.2.178

Reputation, reputation, reputation! O! I have lost my reputation.

O 2.3.264

Sweet, sweet, sweet poison for the age's tooth.

KJ 1.1.213

O dark, dark, dark, amid the blaze of noon.

Milton

All changed, changed utterly:
A terrible beauty is born.

Yeats

Curiosity is almost, almost, the definition of frivolity.

Ortega y Gasset

It is possible, possible, possible. It must be possible.

W. Stevens

Shakespeare used the epizeuxis shamelessly in certain of his plays, particularly in *King Lear.* "Then, kill, kill, kill, kill, kill, kill." "Howl howl howl howl!" "Never, never, never, never, never!" Eliot was having some fun with this tendency when he wrote, "O O O O that Shakespearian Rag."

To lessen the risks involved in epizeuxis, writers, including Shakespeare, often place a word or two before the repetition is made: **diacope**. Frequently the interposing words are qualifiers: adjectives between repeated nouns, adverbs between repeated verbs.

> Company, villainous company, hath been the spoil of me.
>   Shakespeare, 1 H IV 3.3.10

> Words, words, mere words, no matter from the heart.
>   T&C 5.3.109

> O villain, villain, smiling, damned villain!
>   Ham. 1.5.106

> Tomorrow, and tomorrow, and tomorrow...
>   Mac. 5.5.19

> A horse! a horse! my kingdom for a horse!
>   R III 5.4.7

> Put out the light, and then put out the light.
>   O 5.2.7

Words, mere words, you villain, damned smiling villain; put out the lights and then put out the lights before your company, your villainous company, is the ruin of me. (We'll talk about the horse tomorrow.)

VIII

Repetition Again

GERTRUDE STEIN, long after she left Oakland, summed up her philosophy of life memorably: "There ain't any answer. There ain't going to be any answer. There never has been an answer. That's the answer." If she had said simply "Life doesn't make sense," her remark would not have been remembered, for people—rightly or wrongly—say that about life all the time.

Her statement is most striking in its repetition of words from one sentence to another. The most elaborate terminology for figures of repetition was designed to deal with just such a passage as Stein's. The figures are defined by where in the successive sentences or clauses the repeated word or phrase appears. To begin three sentences with "There" (or two with "There ain't") is an **anaphora**.

> He maketh me to lie down in green pastures: he leadeth me beside the still waters. He restoreth my soul: he leadeth me in the paths of righteousness for his name's sake.
>
> Ps. 23:2

> That day is a day of wrath, a day of trouble and distress, a day of wasteness and desolation, a day of darkness and gloominess, a day of clouds and thick darkness.
>
> Zeph. 1:15

> Blessed are the poor in spirit: for theirs is the kingdom of heaven. Blessed are they that mourn: for they shall be comforted. Blessed are the meek for they shall inherit the earth.
>
> Matt. 5:3

Through me the way unto the woeful city,
Through me the way to eternal woe,
Through me the way among people lost.

                                             Dante

This royal throne of kings, this scepter'd isle,
This earth of majesty, this seat of Mars...
This blessed plot, this earth, this realm, this England.
                              Shakespeare, R II 2.1.40

   Mad world! Mad kings! Mad composition!

                                        KJ 2.1.561

Was ever woman in this humor woo'd?
Was ever woman in this humor won?

                                     R III 1.2.229

Some mute unglorious Milton here may rest
Some Cromwell guiltless of his country's blood

                                             Gray

   Everything is good when it leaves the hands of the Creator;
everything degenerates in the hands of man.

                                          Rousseau

   She was not quite what you would call refined. She was not
quite what you would call unrefined. She was the kind of
person that keeps a parrot.

                                       Mark Twain

   They streamed aboard over three gangways, they streamed
in urged by faith and the hope of paradise, they streamed in
with a continuous tramp and shuffle of bare feet without a
word, a murmur or a look back.

                                           Conrad

   We shall not flag or fail. We shall go on to the end. We shall
fight in France, we shall fight on the seas and oceans, we shall
fight with growing confidence and growing strength in the air,
we shall defend our island, whatever the cost may be, we shall
fight on the beaches, we shall fight on the landing grounds, we
shall fight in the fields and in the streets, we shall fight in the
hills; we shall never surrender.

                                         Churchill

To end four sentences with "answer" (or two with "any answer") is an **epistrophe**.

O Israel, trust thou in the Lord: he is their help and their shield. O house of Aaron, trust in the Lord: he is their help and their shield. Ye that fear the Lord, trust in the Lord: he is their help and their shield.

Ps. 115:9

When I was a child, I spake as a child, I understood as a child, I thought as a child: but when I became a man, I put away childish things.

1 Cor. 13:11

The grove of Angita lamented you,
The glassy watered Fuccinus lamented you,
All limpid lakes lamented you.

Virgil

If you the sea held, I would follow you, my wife, until me also the sea held.   Ovid

For truth is one, and right is ever one.

Spenser

Unhappy spirits that fell with Lucifer,
Conspired against our God with Lucifer,
And are forever damned with Lucifer

Marlow

I'll have my bond!
Speak not against my bond!
I have sworn an oath that I will have my bond.

Shakespeare, MV 3.3.4

Julia: They do not love that do not show their love.
Lucetta: O! they love least that let men know their love.

TGV 1.2.31

Why I should fear I know not,
Since guiltiness I know not; but yet I feel I fear.

O 5.2.38

Poetry is certainly something more than good sense, but it must be good sense...just as a palace is more than a house but it must be a house.   Coleridge

Selfishness is not living as one wishes to live. It is asking others to live as one wishes to live.

Macaulay

Men have never been good, they are not good, they never will be good.   Barth

If we began successive sentences with "there" and ended them with "answer," we would be using **symploce**.

Cursed be he that removeth his neighbor's landmark: and all the people shall say, Amen. Cursed be he that maketh the blind to wander out of the way: and all the people shall say, Amen....Cursed be he that lieth with any manner of beast: and all the people shall say, Amen.

Deut. 27:16

Are they Hebrews? So am I. Are they Israelites? So am I. Are they of the seed of Abraham? So am I.

2 Cor. 11:22

Who are they who have so often broken treaties? The Carthaginians. Who are they who have waged war with such atrocious cruelty? The Carthaginians. Who are they who have laid Italy to waste? The Carthaginians. Who are they who pray for pardon? The Carthaginians.

Cicero

Son: How will my mother for a father's death
    Take on with me, and ne'er be satisfied!
Father: How will my wife for slaughter of my son
    Shed seas of tears, and ne'er be satisfied!
King Henry: How will the country for these woeful chances
    Misthink the King, and not be satisfied!

Shakespeare, 3 H VI 2.5.103

If thou hast any sound, or use of voice,
Speak to me.

If there be any good thing to be done,
That may to thee do ease and grace to me,
Speak to me.

Ham. 1.1.128

I'll tell you who Time ambles withal, who Time trots withal,
who Time gallops withal, and who he stands still withal.

AYLI 3.2.309

There are, of course, more forms of repetition than are dreamt of in Gertrude Stein's philosophy. We could end a sentence or clause with the same word or phrase with which we began it: **epanalepsis**. (A question for which there is no answer is still a question, but an answer for which there is no question is no answer.)

Rejoice in the Lord always: and again I say, Rejoice.
Phil. 4:4

Nothing can be created out of nothing.
Lucretius

Poor Cinna wants to appear and is poor.
Martial

Judges must be many in number, for a few will always do the will of a few. Machiavelli

Bold was the challenge as he himself was bold.
Spenser

The thoughts are but overflowings of the mind, and the tongue is but a servant of the thoughts. Sidney

Rhetoric is either very good or stark naught; there is no medium in rhetoric. Selden

Blood hath bought blood, and blows have answer'd blows;
Strength match'd with strength, and power confronted power.
Shakespeare, KJ 2.1.329

Men of few words are the best men.
H V 3.2.40

Cassius from bondage will deliver Cassius.

JC 1.3.90

Kings it makes gods, and meaner creatures kings.

R III 5.2.24

Once more unto the breach, dear friends, once more.

H V 3.1.1

It takes time to ruin a world, but time is all it takes.
Fontenelle

Common sense is not so common

Voltaire

Injury, violation, exploitation, annihilation, cannot be wrong in themselves, for life essentially presupposes injury, violation, exploitation, and annihilation.

Nietzsche

Do not despair, not even over the fact that you do not despair.   Kafka

Whistling to keep up courage is good practice for whistling.
Haskins

Hugo was a madman who believed he was Hugo.

Cocteau

The use of an epanalepsis to mark off a whole passage is called an **inclusio**.

What doth it profit, my brethren, though a man say he hath faith, and have not works? Can faith save him? If a brother or sister be naked, and destitute of daily food, And one of you say unto them, Depart in peace, be ye warmed and filled; notwithstanding ye give them not those things which are needful to the body; what doth it profit?

James 2:14

Do not weep maiden, for war is kind.
Because your love turned wild hands toward the day
And the affrighted steed ran on alone,
Do not weep.
War is kind.   S. Crane

O hidden under the dove's wing, hidden under the turtle's
  breast,
Under the palmtree at noon, under the running water
At the still point of the turning world. O hidden.

Eliot

    The epanalepsis tends to make the sentence or clause in
which it occurs stand apart from its surroundings. We can,
however, just as easily tie it to its surroundings by having its
last word or phrase repeated in the first word or phrase in the
subsequent sentence. This is **anadiplosis**. (I cannot see how I
can use the Stein quote to give an example of such an
anadiplosis; anadiplosis is, nonetheless, easy to understand as
the following examples show; the following examples show, in
particular, how useful this figure is.)

I will lift up mine eyes unto the hills, from whence cometh
my help. My help cometh from the Lord which made heaven
and earth.   Ps. 121:1

Our feet shall stand within thy gates, O Jerusalem.
Jerusalem is builded as a city that is compact together:

Ps.122:2

Therefore shall his calamity come suddenly; suddenly shall
he be broken without remedy.

Prov. 6:15

Does the silk worm expend her yellow labours for thee? For
thee does she undo herself?

Tourneur

Death, as the Psalmist saith, is certain to all; all shall die.

Shakespeare, 2 H IV 3.2.41

Who has not the spirit of his age, of his age has all the
unhappiness.

Voltaire

All men that are ruined are ruined on the side of their
natural propensities.   E.Burke

When I give I give myself.

Whitman

Talent is an adornment; an adornment is also a conceal-
ment.

Nietzsche

Everything that can be said, can be said clearly.

Wittgenstein

Sometimes an author will use repeated anadiplosis,
creating a chain-like progression to his writing: **gradatio**.

Tell ye your children of it, and let your children tell their
children, and their children another generation. That which the
palmerworm hath left hath the locust eaten; and that which the
locust hath left hath the cankerworm eaten; and that which the
cankerworm hath left hath the caterpiller eaten.

Joel 1:3

We glory in tribulations also: Knowing that tribulation
worketh patience; And patience, experience; and experience,
hope: And hope maketh not ashamed

Rom. 5:3

I did not say this, without making a formal proposal to that
effect; I did not make that proposal without undertaking the
embassy, nor undertake the embassy without persuading the
Thebans.   Demosthenes

The boy is the most powerful of all the Hellenes; for the
Hellenes are commanded by the Athenians, the Athenians by
myself, myself by the boy's mother, and the mother by her
boy.   Themistocles

Men into stones therewith he could transmew,
And stones to dust, and dust to nought at all.

Spenser

Then everything includes itself in power,
Power into will, will into appetite;
And appetite, an universal wolf,
So doubly seconded with will and power,

Must make perforce a universal prey,
And last eat up himself.
Shakespeare, T&C 1.3.119

No sooner met, but they looked; no sooner looked but they
loved; no sooner loved but they sighed; no sooner sighed but
they asked one another the reason; no sooner knew the reason
but they sought the remedy.
AYLI 5.2.37

My conscience hath a thousand several tongues,
And every tongue brings in a several tale,
And every tale condemns me for a villain.
R III 5.3.194

Labor and care are rewarded with success, success produces
confidence, confidence relaxes industry, and negligence ruins
the reputation which diligence had raised.
Johnson

All our knowledge brings us nearer to our ignorance,
All our ignorance brings us nearer to death,
But nearness to death no nearer to God.
Eliot

The stairlike progression of the gradatio can also be
achieved by arranging a series of items in ascending importance
(or descending if the intended effect is ironic): **auxesis**.

Blessed is the man that walketh not in the counsel of the
ungodly, nor standeth in the way of sinners, nor sitteth in the
seat of the scornful.   Ps. 1:1

Let this mind be in you, which was also in Christ Jesus:
Who, being in the form of God, thought it not robbery to be
equal with God: But made himself of no reputation, and took
upon him the form of a servant, and was made in the likeness
of men: And being found in fashion as a man, he humbled
himself, and became obedient unto death, even the death of
the cross.   Phil. 2:5

It is a sin to bind a Roman citizen, a crime to scourge him,
little short of the most unnatural murder to put him to death;

what then shall I call this crucifixion?

Cicero

Pleasure might cause her to read, reading might make her
    know,
Knowledge might pitie winne, and pitie grace obtain.

Sidney

Since brass, nor stone, nor earth, nor boundless sea,
But sad mortality o'er-sways their power...
How with this rage shall beauty hold a plea,
Whose action is no stronger than a flower?

Shakespeare, S 65.1

Nurse, O my love is slain, I saw him go
O'er the white Alps alone; I saw him I,
Assailed, fight, taken, stabbed, bleed, fall, and die.

Donne

What shall point out them,
When they shall bow, and kneel, and fall down flat
To kisse those heaps, which now they have in trust?

Herbert

Some have at first for Wits, then Poets past,
Turn'd Critics next, and prov'd plain fools at last

Pope

If once a man indulges himself in murder, very soon he
comes to think little of robbing; and from robbing he comes
next to drinking and Sabbath-breaking, and from that to
incivility and procrastination.

DeQuincey

As useful as these figures are, as common as they are in
ordinary practice, the names are almost impossible to keep
separate, even for someone who is aware of the Greek roots
from which they are constructed. (And please be advised I
have omitted almost all the terms involving repetition in
middles.) One eighteenth century handbook gamely offered its
readers the following jingle:

Anaphora gives more Sentences on Head;
As readily appears to that read.

Epistrophe more Sentences doth close
With the same Words, whether in Verse or Prose
Symploce joins these Figures both together,
And from both join'd makes up itself another.
Epanalepsis Words doth recommend
The same at the Beginning and the End.
Anadiplosis ends the former Line
With what the next does for its first design.

A peculiar form of repetition is a **palindrome** in which the second half of the sentence repeats the letters of the first half in the opposite order. In other words, the sentence reads the same forwards or backwards. So James Joyce will attribute to Napoleon the statement, "Madam, able was I ere I saw Elba." Or how about "A man, a plan, a canal, Panama!"

This would seem to be just an amusing linguistic curiosity, an inverse repetition at the level of spelling. However, if we do the same thing at the level of words, then we find an interesting repetitive figure that often governs an antithesis: **epanados**. (Handbook writers who like nice distinctions will reserve the name **antimetabole** for an epanados which is also an antithesis.)

Woe unto them that call evil good, and good evil; that put darkness for light, and light for darkness; that put bitter for sweet, and sweet for bitter!

Isa. 5:20

The sabbath was made for man, and not man for the sabbath.

Mark 2:27

Ye have not chosen me, but I have chosen you.

John 15:16

The man is not of the woman; but the woman of the man. Neither was the man created for the woman; but the woman for the man.

1 Cor. 11:8

Circumstances rule men; men do not rule circumstances.

Herodotus

Every man seeks peace by waging war, but no man seeks war by making peace.

> Augustine

It is not titles that reflect honor on men, but men on their titles.

> Machiavelli

Life is a dream...we sleeping wake and waking sleep.

> Montaigne

If a man will begin with certainties, he shall end in doubts; but if he will be content to begin with doubts he shall end in certainties.

> Bacon

Fair is foul, and foul is fair:

> Shakespeare, Mac. 1.1.12

What's mine is yours, and what is yours is mine.

> MM 5.1.539

That he is mad, 'tis true; 'tis true 'tis pity;
And pity 'tis 'tis true.

> Ham. 2.2.97

I wasted time, and now doth time waste me.

> R II 5.5.49

For 'tis a question left us yet to prove,
Whether love lead fortune, or else fortune love.

> Ham. 3.2.194

More safe I sing with mortal voice, unchang'd
To hoarse or mute, though fall'n on evil days,
On evil days though fall'n and evil tongues.

> Milton

A man may devote himself to death and destruction to save a nation; but no nation will devote itself to death and destruction to save mankind.

> Coleridge

They were not forty children conducting themselves like one, but every child was conducting itself like forty.

Dickens

Martyrs create faith, faith does not create martyrs.

Unamuno

In the epanados one is organizing a sentence spatially around a center. Such a spatial technique, with its obvious analogies to painting, can be used to organize larger and larger units of material. This technique is frequently employed in the Bible. A large epanados is called a **chiasmus**, after the Greek name for the letter x (which, after all, is a palindrome reduced to a single letter).

And the Lord said unto Moses, The man shall be surely put to death: all the congregation shall stone him with stones without the camp. And all the congregation brought him without the camp, and stoned him with stones, and he died; as the Lord commanded Moses.

Num. 15:35

Jesus saith unto him, Rise, take up thy bed, and walk. And immediately the man was made whole, and took up his bed, and walked: and on the same day was the sabbath. The Jews therefore said unto him that was cured, It is the sabbath day: it is not lawful for thee to carry thy bed. He answered them, He that made me whole, the same said unto me, Take up thy bed, and walk.

John 5:8

Moreover, it has been argued persuasively that the Abraham story in *Genesis,* the whole of the *Book of Ruth,* as well as many other extended Bible segments are organized this way, as are Shakespeare's *Hamlet* and *Tempest,* Moliere's *Tartuffe,* and the whole of Homer's *Iliad.* And, to use a more homely example, I have found it quite helpful with this book as well.

Conclusion

AFTER THE FIGURES of repetition, there is little left of the distinctions on which this book was built. Little left of the distinctions between figures of omission, addition, substitution, and arrangement. Little left particularly of the distinction between literal and figurative usage. Little left except the guidance they gave us through the jungle of style.

Where did it start to unravel? For me with the discussion of the anthimeria. After having blurred the distinctions of grammar, the anthimeria then turned on our definition of the figure of speech. Or so it seemed to me when we discussed the antiptosis.

Rather than the hendiadys "the sound and the fury" the antiptosis would have required of Faulkner "the sound of fury." Perhaps you, like me, were uncomfortable at calling the antiptosis a figure of speech, strictly speaking. To say "a tower of stone" rather than "a stone tower" does not seem like a deviation from ordinary usage, any more than most of the figures of repetition do.

Early in this book we—no, I—brushed aside the question of how one knows a deviant when he sees one. The difficulty of this question is that there are degrees of deviation. How much deviation is required before we ennoble it with the status of figure? Somehow we have to reshape the question.

The first baseball announcer who shouted uncontrollably "He hit that real good!" might have been consciously violating ordinary usage. Probably not, but perhaps. The double wrench of "real good" does seem to capture well both the violence of the hit and the emotion of the announcer—or at least it might have the first hundred times it was used. But now that hundreds of baseball announcers have each shouted uncontrollably hundreds of times "He hit that real good," it has become commonplace. If "real good" ever was a figure, it is now real dead.

A figure is an unusual choice. Robert Frost claimed that his choosing the road less taken made all the difference. Almost all of us will be taking roads more frequently travelled than Frost's, but they may still be among the less travelled. To choose an "of" phrase instead of an adjective may be to choose a road less taken, but it is well-travelled nonetheless.

In the end we must reject any strict distinction between ordinary usage and the figures. If we do not, language becomes a prison house from which only poets can escape, and they always to be recaptured. The figures become a turning of language against itself, not the realization of its deepest potential. And we, already alienated by science from the world, become aliens within our own consciousness as well.

Finding ourselves at home with language means making appropriate choices, not necessarily unusual ones. Great writing is unusual because it is great, not great because it is unusual. (Pace Joyce.) The figures which are the most unusual are the least useful.

In writing this book I have tried to use every figure of speech which I described (except the praecisio). A number of these I expect never to use again. Yet is is good to feel the full range of choices so that we never again think of language as dead and rigid, an alien thing. Language has all the suppleness of human flesh, and something of its warmth. And that is true whether we choose to follow the strict discipline of the isolcolon or the polymorphous perversity of the anthimeria.

And so the time has come for me to tell you my favorite figure of speech, a figure which I have yet to mention. The figure does appear in some handbook; I didn't invent it for this occasion, I assure you. This figure is the hypozeuxis. A **hypozeuxis** occurs when you could have used a zeugma but didn't. I am afraid there is at least one New York journalist who now uses the hypozeuxis every chance he gets.

98

Abbreviations

WORKS OF SHAKESPEARE
AW *All's Well That Ends Well*
A & C *Antony and Cleopatra*
AYLI *As You Like It*
CE *A Comedy of Errors*
Cor. *Coriolanus*
Cym. *Cymberline*
Ham. *Hamlet*
1 H IV *Henry IV, Part 1*
2 H IV *Henry IV, Part 2*
H V *Henry V*
3 H VI *Henry VI, Part 3*
JC *Julius Caesar*
KJ *King John*
KL *King Lear*
LLL *Love's Labor's Lost*
Mac. *Macbeth*
MM *Measure for Measure*
MV *The Merchant of Venice*
MMW *The Merry Wives of Windsor*
MND *A Midsummer Night's Dream*
MAAN *Much Ado About Nothing*
O *Othello*
R II *Richard II*
R III *Richard III*
R & J *Romeo and Juliet*
RL *Rape of Lucrece*
Tem. *The Tempest*
TA *Timon of Athens*
Tit. *Titus Andronicus*
T & C *Troilus and Cressida*
TN *Twelfth Night*
TGV *Two Gentlemen of Verona*
TNK *Two Noble Kinsmen*
WT *A Winter's Tale*
S *Sonnet*

KING JAMES BIBLE
Acts *Acts*
Amos *Amos*
Cor. *Corinthians*
Col. *Colossians*
Deut. *Deuteronomy*
Exod. *Exodus*
Eccles. *Ecclesiastes*
Ezek. *Ezekiel*
Ezra *Ezra*
Gen. *Genesis*
Isa. *Isaiah*
Josh. *Joshua*
Judg. *Judges*
Jer. *Jeremiah*
John *John*
James *James*
Kings *Kings*
Luke *Luke*
Matt. *Matthew*
Mark *Mark*
Num. *Numbers*
Ps. *Psalms*
Phil. *Philippians*
Ruth *Ruth*
Rom. *Romans*
Rev. *Revelations*
Pet. *Peter*
Sam. *Samuel*
Tim. *Timothy*
Zeph. *Zephaniah*

Glossary/Index

Abusio (ab-úˊ-see-oe) *Another name for catachresis.* 55

Accumulatio (ac-cu-mu-laˊ-ee-oe) *Repetition in other words: "I will not excuse you you shall not be excus'd; excuses shall not be admitted."* 65-67

Anadiplosis (anˊ-a-di-ploˊ-sis) *Repetition of an end at the next beginning: "When I give, I give myself."* 89-90

Anaphora (a-naphˊ-o-ra) *Repetition of beginnings: "Mad world! Mad kings! Mad composition!"* 83-84

Anapodoton (a-na-po-doˊ-ton) *Omission of a clause: "If you only knew."* 34

Anastrophe (a-nasˊ-tro-phee) *Arrangement by reversal of order: "Figures pedantical."* 42-43

Antanaclasis (anˊ-an-a-claˊ-sis) *Repetition in different senses: "Let the dead bury their dead."* 76-77

Anthimeria (anˊ-thi-méˊ-ree-a) *Substitution of one part of speech for another: "he sang his didn't."* 50-51

Antimetabole (anˊ-ti-me-ta-bo-lee) *An* epandos *which is also an* antithesis. 93

Antiptosis (anˊ-tip-toéˊ-sis) *Substitution of a prepositional phrase for an adjective: "tower of strength."* 51-52

Antisthecon (an-tisˊ-the-con) *Substitution of letter(s): "togither."* 23.

Antithesis (an-tithˊ-e-sis) *Repetition by negation: "A man should be mourned at his birth, not his death."* 67-68

Aphaersis (aph-airˊ-e-sis) *Omission of letter(s) at the beginning: "scape."* 22

Apocope (a-poćˊ-o-pee) *Omission of letter(s) from the end: "I ope my lips."* 22

Aporia (aˊ-poe-ree-a) *Talking about not being able to talk about: "I can't tell you how often aporia is used."* 36

Aposiopesis (ap-o-seéˊ-o-pee-sis) *Breaking off as if unable or unwilling to continue: "The fire surrounds them while—I cannot go on."* 34-36

Asyndeton (a-synˊ-de-ton) *The omission of a conjunction: "I came, I saw, I conquered."* 7-10

Asterismos (as-ter-isˊ-mos) *Addition of a word to emphasize what follows: "Behold, the day of wrath is at hand."* 63

Auxesis (aux-eéˊ-sis) *Arrangement in ascending importance: "Pleasure might cause her to read, reading might make her know, knowledge might pity winne, and pity grace obtain."* 91-92

Brachylogia (braˊ-kil-o-gee-a) *Omission of a conjunction between words or phrases (in dis-*

101

tinction from similar omissions between clauses): "Hath not a Jew hands, organs, dimensions, senses, affections, passions?" 21

Catachresis (caṫ -a-chree-sis) *Apparently inappropriate substitution of one word for another, inappropriate because there is not an obviously definable relationship between the two:* "blind mouths." 54-56

Chiasmus (chī -as-mus) Epanados *at the level of the passage.* 95

Congeries (coṅ -ge-ries) *Another name for* accumulatio. 65

Diacope (di-aċ -o-pee) *Repetition with only a word or two between:* "Villain, damned smiling villain." 82

Ellipsis (el-liṗ -sis) *Omission:* "Everybody's friend is nobody's." 27-29

Enallage (e-naſ -la-gee) *Substitution of one grammatical form for another, an effective grammatical mistake:* "We was robbed!" 5, 49-50

Enthymene (eṅ -the-meen) *Omission of a logically implied clause or sentence.* "Gabriel is immortal because Gabriel is an angel." 33

Epanados (e-paṅ -o-dos) *Repetition in the opposite order:* "Fair is foul, and foul is fair." 93-95

Epanalepsis (eṗ -an-a-leṗ -sis) *Repetition of the beginning at the end:* "Common sense is not so common." 87-88

Epanorthosis (eṗ -a-nor-thoe-sis) *Addition by correction:* "The hour cometh, yea, is now come." 68-70

Epenthesis (e-peṅ -the-sis) *Addition of letter(s) to the middle:* "bretheren." 21

Epistrophe (e-piṡ -tro-phee) *Repetition of ends:* "When I was a child, I spake as a child, I understood as a child, I thought as a child." 85-86

Epizeuxis (eṗ -i-zeux-is) *Immediate repetition: Comfort ye, comfort ye, my people."* 80-81

Gradatio (gra-dá -tee-oe) *Repeated* anadiplosis: *"Tribulation worketh patience; and patience, experience; and experience, hope; and hope maketh not ashamed."* 90-91

Hendiadys (hen-dī -a-dis) *A combination of addition, substitution, and usually arrangement; the addition of a conjunction between a word (noun, adjective, verb) and its modifier (adjective, adverb, infinitive), the substition of this word's grammatical form for that of its modifier, and usually rearrangement so that the modifier follows the word:* "furious sound" becomes "sound and fury." 16-17, 25

Hypallage (hy-paſ -la-gee) *Reversal which seems to change the sense:* "waters of the city" becomes "the city of waters." 43-45

Hyperbaton (hy-peṙ -ba-ton) *Misplacement of a single element: About suffering they were never wrong."* 40-42

Hysteron-proteron (hyṡ -te-ron proṫ -e-ron) *Reversal of temporal order:* "Let us die and rush into the heart of battle." 43

Hypozeuxis (hẏ -po-zeux́ -is) *The omision of a* zeugma. 98

Inclusio (in-cloó -see-oe) *Repetition of the beginning of a passage at its end.* 88-89

Isocolon (i-so-có -lon) *Repetition of grammatical forms:* "The bigger they are, the harder they fall." 77-79

Metalepsis (meṫ -a-leṗ -sis) *A* metonymy *apparently involving a double substitution:* "the beards of corn." 19

Metaplasmus (meṫ -a-plaṡ -mus) *Effective misspelling.* 54

102

Metonymy (me-ton´-y-mee) *Substitution of a word for a related word, such as cause for effect, container for contained: "The pen is mightier than the sword."* 52-53

Palindrome (pal´-in-drome) *Repetition of the same letters in opposite order: "Able was I ere I saw Elba."* 93

Paradiastole (par´-a-di-as´-to-lee) *Addition of a disjuntive conjunction: "Not snow, no, nor rain, nor heat, nor night keeps them from accomplishing their appointed rounds."* 13-15

Periphrasis (pe-riph´-ra-sis) *Substitution of more words for less: "I said the thing which was not."* 64-65

Pleonasm (plee´-o-nasm) *Addition of superfluous words: "the inaudible and noiseless foot of time."* 61-63

Ploce (ploe´-see) *Repetition of a word in a general and restricted sense: "more Irish than the Irish."* 77

Polyptoton (po-lyp´-toe-ton) *Repetition of the same word or root in different grammatical functions or forms: "Few men speak humbly of humility."* 74-75

Polysyndeton (pol´-y-syn´-de-ton) *Addition of conjuctions: The horizon narrowed and widened, and dipped and rose."* 11-13

Praecisio (pray-kis´-ee-oe) *Omission of everything.* 36-37

Praeteritio (pret-e-rit´-ee-oe) *The inclusion of something by pretending to omit it: "I will not question the motives of those who seek my impeachment."* 70

Proparalepsis (pro´-par-a-lep´-sis) *Addition of letter(s) to the end: "Eddie."* 22

Prosthesis (pros´-the-sis) *Addition of letters to the beginning: "beweep."* 21

Repetitio (rep-e-tit´-ee-oe) *Irregular repetition of a word or phrase: "Light seeking light doth light of light beguile."* 79-80

Scesis onamaton (skee´-sis o-no-ma´-ton) *Omission of the only verb of a sentence. "Only this and nothing more."* 33

Syllepsis (syl-lep´-sis) *Omission entailing a pun, a combination of ellipsis (usually in its* zeugma *form) and* antanaclasis: *"stain her Honour or her new Brocade."* 31

Symploce (sym-plo´-kee) *Repetition of both beginnings and endings: "Are they Hebrews? So am I. Are they Israelites? So am I. Are they of the seed of Abraham? So am I."* 86-86

Synaloepha (syn-a´-le-pha) *Omission of a vowel and the arrangement of two words into one: "don't."* 22

Syncope (syn-ko´-pee) *Omission of a letter from the middle of a word: "Thou thy wordly task hast done."* 22

Synecdoche (syn-ek´-do-kee) *Substitution of a part for a whole: "A hungry stomach has no ears."* 56-58

Tmesis (tme´-sis) *Arrangement of one word into two: "im possible."* 39

Zeugma (zeug´-ma) *Ellipsis of a verb from one of two or more usually parallel clauses: "Passion lends them power, time means, to meet."* 29-31